Studying Together

A Ready-reference Bible Handbook

By
Mark Finley
Speaker/Director

of the
It Is Written
International Television Ministry
Thousand Oaks, California

A Publication of Hart Research Center

REVISED EDITION

Another Outreach Resource Distributed by
Hart Research Center
P.O. Box 2377
Fallbrook, CA 92088
(760) 723-8082

Project Manager: Richard Dower
Editor/Designer: Nadine Dower
Editorial Assistant: Ernestine Finley
Proofreaders: Rosemary Waterhouse,
                     James Flees
Data Entry: Valmae Lowry
                     Glenda Willis

Litho in USA

ISBN 978-1-878046-08-6

9 781878 046086

Table of Contents

Bible Studies You Can Give

Table of Contents

Bible Studies You Can Give

Practical Christianity

Understanding Churches, Denominations, and other Religious Groups

Foreword

You hold in your hands a goldmine of information. Over 100,000 copies of the first edition of this book are helping people around the world discover new insights from Scripture on sharing the incredible love of Jesus and His rescue plan for this planet.

If there is one thing in Mark Finley's worldwide ministry that stands out above the rest, it is his passion for winning people to Jesus Christ. The information he shares in this resource book is based on tried and tested experience proclaiming the Gospel to tens of thousands of people in North and South America, Europe, and the former Soviet Union.

Remember that information, all by itself, can be dangerous! In fact, it is destructive to God's purposes when presented in a forceful, argumentative manner. But let this information be combined with a life completely surrendered to Jesus Christ. Then add deep, earnest, intercessory prayer for the outpouring of the Holy Spirit in Latter Rain power! As it spreads, the impact on our world will be greater than Pentecost, and our Lord will come!

I pray that a passion for winning people to Jesus Christ will become a driving force in your life too.

Daniel F. Houghton
President
Hart Research Center

Introduction

How to use this Handbook most effectively

This Bible Handbook is especially designed to assist you in studying the beautiful Christ-centered truths of the Bible with your friends and neighbors. It is divided into three main sections:

1. A series of doctrinal Bible studies each followed by the questions asked most often regarding that doctrine with scriptural answers.

2. A series of practical Bible lessons for the daily problems of life.

3. A brief description of various religious groups and denominations with suggestions for approaching them in the spirit of Christ.

You may use this booklet as the basis for a series of Bible studies or as a supplementary aid to studies you are already using. It contains hundreds of Bible texts. Its straightforward Biblical answers will provide you with a wealth of material for studying with others. The Word of God contains life-changing power. The same Holy Spirit which inspired the Bible will accompany you as you present it's precious truths to others. Working through you, the Spirit will apply the truths of scriptures in other lives. You may feel inefficient yet the Holy Spirit will be your efficiency. You may feel ignorant yet the Holy Spirit will be your wisdom. You may feel weak yet the Holy Spirit will be your strength. It is written, "There is no limit to the usefulness of one who, by putting self aside, makes room for the working of the Holy Spirit upon his heart" *(Desire of Ages, p. 250.)* The Spirit of God will richly reward you as you enter into the most wonderful work in the world, studying the Bible with others. There will be souls in the Kingdom of God as a direct result of your ministry. *Studying Together* is only a tool. *You* are the key ingredient our Lord desires to use to win souls—His Spirit will enable you to do it.

Section I

Bible studies you can give, with specific answers to some of the most commonly asked questions

This section contains thirty-two doctrinal Bible Studies. Each study presents one aspect of Bible truth. Texts are linked together in a systematic way so each link in the chain of truth carefully fits with the succeeding link. Text summaries follow each Bible reference so you will know clearly what is in the text.

Rightly understood, Bible doctrines are clear. Questionable passages must always be harmonized with those that are plain. No Bible doctrine is built around a single text— to understand Bible truth the totality of scripture must be considered. You will find straightforward Bible answers to sometimes difficult questions immediately following each doctrinal Bible Study.

Section II

Practical Christianity: answers meeting inmost needs

The problems of life find practical answers in the Word of God. This section provides God's answers to our daily difficulties. It reveals a Christ who is not far distant but one who is near at hand—a Christ who is both interested in and capable of solving our daily problems.

Section III

Understanding denominations, churches, and other religious groups

The section presents a brief background of each group, discussing their major teachings with practical suggestions in reaching people in that particular group. Since this is a Bible *handbook* and not library encyclopedic reference work on world religions, we are intentionally brief. I have designed these comments so they are concrete, specific, practical, and easy to put into practice as you share Jesus and His truth with your friends. I pray that this section will enable you to understand the essence of what each group believes and give you direction in reaching them for Him.

Mark Finley
It Is Written
International Television Ministry

Bible Studies You Can Give

With specific answers to some of the
most commonly asked questions

The Bible

2 Pet. 1:21	Holy men of God spoke as they were moved by the Holy Ghost.
2 Tim. 3:16	All scripture is inspired by God.
Ps. 119:160	God's word is true from the beginning.
Ps. 12:6,7	God has preserved His word through the centuries.
Matt. 24:35	God's word is eternal.
Rom. 15:4	One of the purposes of God's word is to give us hope.
2 Tim. 3:15	The scriptures make us wise unto salvation.
Jn. 5:39	The scriptures reveal Jesus as Saviour.
2 Tim. 2:15	As we study we must rightly divide.
Jn. 16:13	Jesus has sent the Holy Spirit to guide us into all truth.
1 Cor. 2:13	As we open our hearts to the Spirit's influence and compare spiritual things with spiritual, God will guide us.
Isa. 28:9,10	As we compare scripture with scripture, we will discover truth.
Jn. 17:17	Truth is contained in God's word.
Jn. 7:17	As we approach God's word with an open mind, He will guide us. *(See Rev. 22:18-20.)*

Facts About the Bible

The Bible contains 66 Books written by 44 authors. It was written over a 1500-year period of time.

Evidence of the Bible's inspiration includes:

Prophecy—See the following: Babylon *(Isa. 13: 19-22)*, Tyre *(Ezek. 26:3-5)*, Sidon *(Ezek. 28:21-23)*, Cyrus *(Isa. 44:28, 45:1)*, Medo-Persia & Greece *(Dan. 8:20,21)*, and Jesus' Birthplace *(Mic. 5:2)*.

Archaeology—*Moabite Stone* discovered in 1868 at Dibon, Jordan, confirming Moabite attacks on Israel as recorded in *2 Kings 1 & 3*.
The Lachish Letters, discovered 1932-1938, 24 miles north of Beersheba, describing the attack of Nebuchadnezzar on Jerusalem in 586 B.C.
The Dead Sea Scrolls were discovered in 1948. They date back to 150-170 B.C. and contain all or parts of the Old Testament books except the book of Esther. They confirm the Bible's accuracy.
Cyrus' Cylinder records Cyrus' overthrow of Babylon and his subsequent deliverance of the Jewish captives.
The Rosetta Stone discovered in 1799, in Egypt, by Napoleon's scientists, was written in three languages—hieroglyphics, demotic, and Greek. It unlocked the mystery of understanding hieroglyphics. Understanding hieroglyphics helps to confirm the authenticity of the Bible.

Cohesive unity—Evidence of the Bible's inspiration also includes its cohesive unity. In more than 3000 places the Bible declares itself inspired *(2 Pet. 1:21)*. It does not contradict itself. It is either inspired by God or a fraud.

Accuracy—Certainly it is inconceivable that a Book so accurate through the centuries could be considered anything less than inspired by God.

Christ revealed—The greatest evidence of the Bible's inspiration is evidenced in the Christ it reveals and the changes in those who study it (see *Jn. 5:39, Acts 4:12, Matt. 11:26-28*).

God (A Character of Love)

Ps. 90:2	From everlasting to ever-lasting (eternal).
Dan. 2:20	All powerful and all wise.
Dan. 2:21	He sets up and takes down kings.
Isa. 46:10	He declares the end from the beginning.
Isa. 45:21	Only He has the ability to reveal the future.
Ps. 33:6,9	The all powerful Creator. *(Gen. 1:1)*
Ex. 34:6,7	Longsuffering, gracious and merciful.
Jer. 31:3	Draws us with loving kindness.
Ps. 24:1	The Owner of all the world.
Ps. 19:1	Even the heavens reveal His glory.
Ps. 34:1-4	He invites us to praise Him and He will deliver us from our fears.
Isa. 41:10	He promises to strengthen us in all our difficulties.
Isa. 43:1-3	He promises to be with us in the deep waters and fiery trials of life.
Heb. 13:5	He promises never to leave or forsake us.

Origin of Evil

1 Jn. 4:8	God is love.
Matt. 13:24-28	An enemy of God and man sows evil tares in the field of the world.
Ezek. 28:12-17	Lucifer was once a beautiful angel created by God with freedom of choice whose pride led him to rebel.
Isa. 14:12-14	Lucifer desired to exalt his throne above God's. He desired to make laws rather than observe them.
Rev. 12:7-9	War broke out in heaven. Satan and his angels fought against Jesus and His angels.
Lk. 10:18	Satan was cast out of heaven.
Gen. 1:27-31	God created man in His image placing him in a magnificent garden home.
Gen. 3:1-7	Satan led Adam and Eve to mistrust God by openly defying His command.
Isa. 59:1,2	Sin separates us from God.
Rom. 6:23	The ultimate result of disobedience is death.
Jer. 17:9	The nature of the human race changed as the result of mankind's disobedience his nature became sinful.
Rom. 5:12; 6:16	The entire human race plunged into guilt, disobedience and sin.

Heb. 2:14-17	Jesus took man's nature. Faced man's temptations and was victorious *(Heb. 4:15).*
Rom. 5:17-19	Jesus redeemed Adam's failure.
Rom. 3:24,25	Through Jesus salvation is ours as a gift.
Isa. 41:13	Jesus is with us in all of our troubles today. He comforts us in all of our heartaches.
Ezek. 28:17,18	Satan will be completely destroyed at the end.
Rev. 21:1-5	Our God will establish a new heavens and a new earth.
Nah. 1:9	Sin will never rear its ugly head a second time.

Prophecies of the Messiah

Mic. 5:2	Birthplace—Bethlehem *(Lk. 2:1-7).*
Isa. 7:14	Virgin Birth *(Matt. 1:23).*
Gen. 49:8-10	Jesus lineage through Judah *(Lk. 1:30-32).*
Num. 24:17	A star shall arise out of Judah *(Matt. 2:1,2).*
Isa. 61:1-3	The ministry of the Messiah predicted in advance *(Lk. 4:16-21).*
Ps. 55:12,13	Betrayed by a friend *(Matt. 26:47-50).*
Zech. 11:12,13	Betrayed for 30 pieces of silver, money used to buy a Potter's field *(Matt. 27:3-9).*
Isa. 53:4-7	Led as a lamb to the slaughter *(Jn. 1:29; Acts 8:32-35).*
Ps. 22:16	Jesus' hands and feet pierced, not stoned *(Lk. 23:33; 24:39).*
Ps. 22:18	Garments parted, soldiers cast dice for His cloak *(Matt. 27:35).*
Ps. 22:1	Jesus' last words, "My God, my God, why hast thou forsaken me?" *(Matt. 27:46).*
Ps. 34:20	Not a bone broken *(Jn. 19:36).*
Isa. 53:9	Buried in a rich man's grave *(Matt. 27:57-60).*
Ps. 16:10	Resurrected from the dead *(Matt. 28:2-7).*

The Divinity of Christ

Matt. 1:23	Immanuel "God is with us."
Jn. 1:1	Word was God *(verse 14)*, Word (Jesus) made flesh.
Jn. 17:5,24	Jesus existed with the father before the foundation of this world.
Jn. 8:58	Jesus declared He was the self-existent one—the "I Am," that He existed before Abraham.
Ex. 3:14	"I Am" is the name of God.
Lk. 5:20-24	Jesus forgave sins, only God can do that.
Jn. 20:28	Thomas testified that He was both Lord and God.
Heb. 1:5-9	The Father addresses the Son as God.
Isa. 9:6	Jesus is everlasting and eternal.
Mic. 5:2	Christ's goings forth have been from everlasting.
1 Tim. 6:15,16	Jesus has immortality.
Rev. 1:18	Jesus is the first and last with keys to the grave.
Phil. 2:5-12	Jesus voluntarily gives up His divine privilege to become our Saviour.

A Commonly Asked Question Regarding the Divinity of Christ

Doesn't the Bible teach that Jesus was the "first born" of all creation and as such a created being not co-existent with the Father from eternity?

The text in question is *Col. 1:15* which calls Jesus the first born of every creature. The Greek word here is *prototokos* meaning the pre-eminent one—the one who has the privileges and prerogatives of God. Jesus is first born not in the sense of time but in the sense of privilege. All the privileges of the first born are His. David was the eighth son of Jesse, yet called the first born. Jesus declared that He was the "I Am" *(Jn. 8:58)* meaning the self-existent one. He said, "before Abraham was, I Am." Isaiah the prophet calls Him the everlasting Father *(Isa. 9:6)*. Micah declares that His origin is from everlasting *(Mic. 5:2)*. John affirms, "In the beginning was the word and the word was with God and the word was God." *(Jn. 1:1)*. Jesus had the privileges and prerogatives of God. He thought equality with God not a thing to be grasped while the world was lost, so He voluntarily left heaven to become a man. He dwelt in human flesh, fought temptations' battles as we fight them, and overcame in our behalf *(Phil. 2:5-11, Heb. 2:14,17)*.

Salvation

1 Jn. 4:8,9	God is love. Love prompted Him to redeem us.
Gen. 1:27-31	God created human beings in His image.
Gen. 3:8	Sin destroys our fellowship with God so we run from His presence *(Isa. 59:1,2)*.
Rom. 6:23	Separated from God we deserve to die eternally.
Rom. 3:23	All have sinned and are under the penalty of death.
Rom. 5:18,19	Adam brought death, Jesus brings life.
Gal. 3:13	Jesus bore our curse.
Heb. 2:8,9	Jesus experienced death for us.
2 Cor. 5:21	Jesus became sin (took its penalty for us).
Acts 3:19	As we repent, He forgives.
1 Jn. 1:9	As we confess, He pardons.
Rom. 8:1	Receiving Jesus, we are no longer condemned.
Eph. 2:8	Through grace by faith we are saved.
Jn. 1:12	As we receive Him by faith we become sons of God.
1 Jn. 5:11-13	Believing in Him, we receive the gift of eternal life.
Jn. 3:16	Salvation is a present experience and gift of God for all who believe.

A Commonly Asked Question Regarding Salvation

Doesn't the Bible teach that once you come to Jesus you can never lose your salvation? *Jn. 10:28* states "and I give unto them eternal life and they shall never perish, neither shall any man pluck them out of mine hand."

Coming to Jesus, accepting His forgiveness by faith, receiving His grace, we receive the gift of eternal life *(Eph. 2:8, Rom. 3:22-25)*. Salvation is a free gift. It is not something we earn by our obedience. Salvation is by grace through faith. When the Philippian jailer asked, "What must I do to be saved?" Paul responded, "Believe in the Lord Jesus Christ"*(Acts 16:30,31)*. Belief is a function of the will. The same mind which chooses to believe can choose to disbelieve and unbelief leads to spiritual death *(Heb. 3:12-14)*. If we do not hold our confidence in God to the end, we will develop a heart of unbelief. "He that endures until the end shall be saved"*(Matt. 24:13)*. We are saved only if we keep in memory what was preached and live the life of faith *(1 Cor. 15:1,2)*. It is always possible to return to the old life of sin, have our names blotted out of the Book of Life and be eternally lost *(2 Pet. 2:19-22, Rev. 3:5, 1 Cor. 9:27)*. The word which Paul uses for cast away in *1 Cor. 9:27* is the same word that is used in *Jer. 6:30* for those who are burned and ultimately lost. In *Jn. 10:28,* when we come to Jesus we receive eternal life. Just as His coming into the heart by faith brings life, our unbelief brings spiritual death. We cannot be unborn, but we can die. Nothing can take us from His hand except our own choice.

Confession and Forgiveness

Mic. 7:18,19	God willingly pardons.
Heb. 8:12	God remembers our sins no more.
Acts 3:19	He blots out our transgressions.
1 Jn. 1:9	He freely forgives.
Isa. 44:22	As a thick cloud, He blots out our transgressions.
Isa. 43:25	God will not remember our sins.
Ps. 32:1	Forgiveness brings happiness.
Isa. 55:7	God abundantly pardons.
Neh. 9:17	Even in our rebellion, He is a God ready to pardon.
Col. 1:14	Forgiveness is rooted in the very character of God.
Ps. 103:3	God's forgiveness is complete. He forgives all of our iniquities.
Lk. 7:47	He forgives our many sins.
Eph. 4:32	We forgive one another because He has forgiven us.
2 Cor. 2:7,9	To be Christlike is to forgive.

Europe's Future Revealed

Dan. 2:1	Nebuchadnezzer dreams a dream which He cannot remember.
Dan. 2:2-11	The King's wise men were unable to either recall or explain the dream.
Dan. 2:16	Daniel pleads for time to pray.
Dan. 2:21-23	God reveals the dream to Daniel.
Dan. 2:28	There is a God in heaven who reveals secrets.
Dan. 2:29,30	The dream reveals what shall come to pass hereafter.

The Dream Revealed

Dan. 2:31	A great image.
Dan. 2:32-36	Head of gold, breast and arms of silver, thighs of brass, legs of iron, feet of iron and clay. Stone smashes the image to the ground.

The Dream Interpreted

Dan. 2:36	God and Daniel "We" shall tell the interpretation.
Dan. 2:38	Nebuchadnezzer "you are the head of gold." The Babylonian empire ruled the world from 605 B.C. to 539 B.C.
Dan. 2:39	Another kingdom inferior to thee.
Dan. 5:28,30-31	The Medes and Persians overthrew the Babylonians.

Isa.44:27,28; *45:1*	The amazing prediction that Cyrus, general of Medo-Persia would attack and overthrow Babylon allowing God's people freedom. (This prophecy was made over 100 years in advance.)
Dan. 2:39	*(Last part)* Another third kingdom of brass.
Dan. 8:20,21	Greece conquered Medo-Persia. (This prophecy was made 200 years in advance.) The Medes and Persians ruled from 539 B.C. to 331 B.C. The Greeks ruled from 331 to 168 B.C.
Dan. 2:40	The fourth kingdom strong as iron represents Rome. Rome ruled from 168 B.C. to 351 A.D.
Dan. 2:41	The Empire shall be divided. Rome was! The divided empire would be partly strong and partly broken.
Dan. 2:43	Kings and queens of Europe attempt to unite the empire through inter-marriage, political intrigue, or war.
Dan. 2:44	God ultimately establishes His kingdom.
Dan. 2:45	The Rock cut out without hands is Jesus' kingdom.
Ps. 2:8,9	Heathens are broken to pieces.
Tit. 2:11-13	Blessed hope and glorious appearing.

Second Coming (Manner)

Jn. 14:1-3   Jesus promised He would return.

Acts 1:9-11   Angels confirmed His promise and testified to its truthfulness.

Jude 14   Enoch, the seventh from Adam, prophesied of our Lord's return.

Ps. 50:3   David declares "Our Lord shall come." There are over 1500 prophecies of Jesus' Second Coming recorded in the Bible. For every prophecy of His first coming mentioned in the Old Testament, there are eight predicting His Second Coming. The return of our Lord is mentioned one in every 25 verses in the New Testament.

Rev. 1:7   When Jesus returns every eye shall see Him.

Matt. 24:27   His return shall be like lightning flashing across the sky.

1 Thess. 4:16,17   It will be an audible event. The righteous dead will be resurrected and along with the righteous living caught up in the sky.

1 Cor. 15:51-54   God will clothe His people with immortality.

Matt. 16:27   His return shall be a glorious event. He comes with His reward.

Rev. 6:14-17	The unrighteous wicked fear His coming and cry for the rocks to fall upon them.
Matt. 13:37-43	The evil are purged out of His kingdom by fire and the righteous saved through all eternity.
Isa. 25:9	The righteous are delighted to see Him come. They joyfully exclaim "Lo, this is our God..."
Rev. 19:11-16	As King of Kings leading the armies of heaven, He returns as triumphant Lord.
Titus 2:13	His coming is called the "Blessed Hope" of a lost mankind.
Rev. 22:11,12, 17-20	Jesus' final invitation to prepare for His soon return.

Commonly Asked Questions Regarding Jesus' Second Coming

Isn't Jesus coming secretly? Doesn't the Bible say, "There will be two in the field, one taken and one left" *(Matt. 24:40)*.

The Bible makes it abundantly plain that Jesus' coming is not a secret event *(Rev. 1:7, Ps. 50:3, 1 Thess. 4:16,17, Matt. 24:27)*. When the Bible speaks of those being left, it does not say they will be left alive on earth. The extended passage in *Lk. 17:26-37* describes the event in detail. In Noah's day there were two classes, "one taken (saved), one left (destroyed by the flood)*(verse 27)*. In Lot's day there were two classes, (one taken out of the city and saved, one left in the city and consumed by the fire). It will be similar when Jesus comes *(Lk. 17:30-37)*. One class will be taken to heaven with Jesus and the other class will be destroyed. In *Lk. 17:37*, the question is raised, "Where, Lord? Where are these people left." The Bible answer is plain, "Whithersoever the body is, there the eagles will be gathered together." *Rev. 19:11-18* clarifies the point that the wicked are destroyed when Jesus comes, (see also *2 Thess. 1:7-9, 2:8*)

Doesn't the Bible teach Jesus is coming as a thief (*1 Thess. 5:2*)?

Each Bible reference to Jesus coming as a thief, is in reference to the unexpected time of Jesus' coming, not the manner of His coming. He comes quickly as a thief, unexpectedly as a thief, but in glorious splendor as lightning in triumphant glory (see *Matt. 24:42-44, 1 Thess. 5:1-5, Matt. 24:27*).

Do God's people live through the coming tribulation or are they raptured before the tribulation?

The experiences of ancient Israel were examples given by God for His people living at the close of time. Just as Israel was delivered from Egyptian bondage after the plagues, so God's church will be protected through the plagues and be delivered from the hand of the oppressor *(1 Cor. 10:11; Ps. 91; 46)*. Shadrach, Meshach, and Abednego entered the flames when they refused to yield to the universal death decree of Babylon's King. In those flames God miraculously delivered them. Their death-defying faith faced the flames *(Dan. 3:16-28)*. He comes as a thief after the plagues *(Rev. 16:15)*. What sense would it make to declare "Behold I come as a thief after six plagues are already poured out" if He had already come as a thief before they were poured out? *Rev. 15:8* emphatically declares "No man can enter the (heavenly) temple until the plagues are completed. *2 Thess. 2:1-3* makes it plain that the anti-christ is revealed before Jesus comes and is destroyed by the brightness of His coming *(2 Thess. 2:8)*.

Does the Bible teach that the righteous receive their reward when they are raptured at the beginning of a seven-year tribulation but the unrighteous are destroyed at the end of the seven-year tribulation?

The parables of Jesus make it plain that the Second Coming of Jesus is a divine climactic event—men and women are either saved or lost. There is no seven-year period to reconsider our lives. Now is the day of salvation *(2 Cor. 6:2)*. In *Matt. 13:30,* both wheat and tares (the righteous and wicked) grow together until the harvest. The righteous are saved and the unrighteous lost. In the parable of the unfaithful servant, there is no second chance. The unfaithful are lost when the Lord of the household comes unexpectedly *(Matt. 24:44-51)*. In the parable of the sheep and goats, men and women are either saved or lost when Jesus comes *(Matt. 25:31-46)*.

Second Coming (Signs)

Matt. 24:3	Jesus disciples ask "What shall be the sign of your coming and the end of the world."
Matt. 24:4,5, 11.24	False religious teachers.
Matt. 24:6,7	Wars and rumors of war.
Rev. 11:18	When the nations are angry, Christ will ultimately destroy those who destroy the earth.
Lk. 21:26	Men's hearts failing with fear.
1 Thess. 5:2,3	Peace talks.
Matt. 24:7	Natural disasters (earthquakes, famines, pestilence).
Matt. 24:12	Rising crime and violence, iniquity.
2 Tim. 3:1-4	Perilous times, moral decadence.
Matt. 24:37-39	Intemperate, morally corrupt.
Jas. 5:1-5	Economic difficulties.
Lk. 21:34	Overwhelmed by cares of this life.
Matt. 24:14	Gospel preached to all the world (see also *Rev. 14:6,7*).
2 Pet. 3:8-10	God chooses to save all.
Matt. 24:48	The evil servant says "My Lord delays His Coming."
Matt. 24:42-44	God's counsel is "Be ready."

Judgment

Rev. 14:6,7	God's final message to mankind pictures judgment.
Rev. 22:12	Since Jesus comes to give out His rewards, there must be a judgment before He comes to determine who receives what reward, when He comes.
Matt. 12:36	Jesus pictured the judgment as future.
Acts 24:25	Paul reasons with Felix of judgment to come.
Dan. 7:9,10	Daniel saw the sitting of the Supreme Court of the Universe and the opening of the judgment.
Eccl. 12:13,14	God will bring every secret thing into judgment.
Heb. 4:13	All things are open unto God.
2 Cor. 5:10	We must all appear before the judgment seat of Christ.
Rom. 14:12	Everyone of us must give account of himself to God.
Ps. 87:6	In the judgment the Lord considers where we were born.
Jer. 2:22	All of our iniquities (sins) are marked before God.
Mal. 3:16	All of our righteous acts prompted by unselfish motives, accomplished through the grace of Christ, are recorded before God.

Rev. 20:12	The basis of judgment is the record of our lives revealed in heaven's record.
Acts 3:19	If we turn from sin in repentance, our sins will be blotted out of God's record in the final judgment.
Rev. 3:5	If we continue in sin, failing to overcome, openly rebelling against God, our names are blotted out of God's record.
Rom. 8:1	The only way to overcome the condemnation of judgment is through Jesus.
Heb. 7:24,25	Our heavenly high Priest is able to save to the uttermost all who come to God through Him.
Jn. 14:26	The Holy Spirit is God's teacher.
Matt. 12:31,32	To reject the convicting, converting, instructing power of the Holy Spirit continually is to commit the unpardonable sin.

Law of God

Ps. 111:7,8	God's commandments are heaven's eternal code of conduct which stands fast forever.
Rom. 3:20	God's law leads us to see our guilt and drives us to Jesus.
Ps. 19:7	God's law is an agency leading us to conversion.
Ps. 19:11	In keeping His commandments, there is a great reward.
Rom. 6:14	We are not "under the law" as a means of salvation. Salvation comes totally and always by grace *(Eph. 2:8)*.
Rom. 6:15	Although we are not under the law, this does not give us liberty to break God's law.
1 Jn. 3:4	Sin is defined as breaking God's law.
Isa. 59:1,2	Sin or breaking God's law leads to separation from God and eternal death *(Rom. 6:23)*.
Rom. 3:28-31	When we are saved by faith we desire to keep God's law *(Heb. 10:7; Jn. 8:29)*.
Jn. 14:15	Love always leads to obedience. Jesus said, "If you love me, keep my commandments."
1 Jn. 2:4,5	He that keepeth not His commandments is a liar and the truth is not in him.
Heb. 8:10	In the new covenant, Jesus writes His law in our hearts.

Ps. 40:8	He places within our hearts the desire to do His will.
Rev. 14:12	God's last day people keep His commandments through faith.
Rev. 12:17	His remnant, like the faithful through the ages, keep His law.

Commonly Asked Questions Regarding The Law of God

Didn't Jesus come to do away with the ten commandments and establish a new commandment of love? What about *Matt. 22:37-40,* "Love God with all your heart and your neighbors as yourself?" Isn't love to God and our neighbors all Jesus requires? These are the new commandments.

It may surprise you to discover that Jesus was summarizing the law as given in the Old Testament. *Deut. 6:5* declares "Love the Lord your God with all your heart." *Lev. 19:18* adds, "Love your neighbor as yourself." The God of the Old Testament was a God of everlasting love *(Jer. 31:3).* In *Matt. 22:40,* Jesus declared, "On these two commands (love to God and fellow man) hang all the laws and the prophets." The first four commandments reveal how human beings tangibly demonstrate their love to their to God. The last six commandments show how they demonstrate their love to their fellow man. "Jesus did not come to destroy the law, but to fulfill it" *(Matt. 5:17).* He revealed how to lovingly keep the law. He came to magnify the meaning of the law *(Isa. 42:21).* Jesus reveals how love is the fulfilling of the law *(Rom. 13:10).* He adds "If you love me, keep my commandments" *(Jn. 14:15).*

Does Paul teach that Christians saved by faith do not have to keep the law?

Paul teaches that Christians are saved not by faith, but by grace through faith. Faith is the hand that takes the salvation freely offered by Jesus. Faith does not lead to disobedience but to obedience. Paul states in no uncertain terms "Do we then make void the law through faith, God forbid"*(Rom. 3:31). Rom. 6:1,14,15* adds,

"Shall we sin (break the law) so grace may abound. God forbid!"

Is it true that in the Old Testament people were saved by keeping the law while in the New Testament, salvation is by grace?

In both the Old and New Testaments, salvation is by grace through faith. God does not have two methods of salvation. *Titus 2:11* affirms, "For the grace of God which bringeth salvation hath appeared unto *all* men." In the Old Testament men and women were saved by the Christ that was to come. Each lamb sacrificed pointed forward to the coming of the Messiah *(Gen. 3:21, Gen. 22:9-13)*. In the New Testament, men and women are saved by the Christ who has come. In one instance faith looked forward to the cross; in the other instance faith looked backward to the cross. Jesus is the only means of salvation *(Acts 4:12)*.

Since we are under the New Covenant, is it really necessary to keep God's law?

The New Covenant is actually older than the Old Covenant. It was given by God Himself in the Garden of Eden when He promised that the Messiah would come to break the deadly hold of Satan upon the human race. The New Covenant contains the promise of redemption from sin through Jesus Christ. He saves us! He writes the principles of the law in our hearts. Love becomes the motivation for obedience. There is a new power in the life *(Heb. 8:10, Ezek. 36:26, Ps. 40:8)*. Under the Old Covenant, Israel promised to obey God's commandments in their own strength. They declared, "all that God says we will do" *(Ex. 19:8; 24:3,7)*. All attempts at external conformity to God's law lead to frustrated defeat. The law which we cannot keep in our own strength condemns us *(Rom. 3:23, 6:23)*. Under the New Covenant, we belong to a new master—Jesus Christ. We have a new heart and a new standing before God *(Jn. 1:12, 2 Cor. 5:17, Rom. 8:1).*

Sabbath

Rev. 14:6,7	God's final message to mankind is a call to worship the Creator.
Rev. 4:11	The basis of all worship is the fact that God created us.
Eph. 3:9	Since Jesus was the active agent in creation, Revelation's final call to worship the Creator is a call to give honor to Jesus.
Ex. 20:8-11	We worship Him as the Creator by keeping His Sabbath.
Gen. 2:1-3	The Sabbath was set apart at creation. God rested upon the seventh day, blessed the seventh day and hallowed it.
Mk. 2:27,28	The Sabbath was given to the human race 2300 years before the existence of the Jews as a memorial for all mankind.
Ezek. 20:12,20	The Sabbath was established for all mankind as a sign between God and His people.
Lk. 4:16	Jesus was a faithful Sabbath keeper.
Matt. 24:20	Jesus predicted the Sabbath would be kept in 70 A.D. at the destruction of Jerusalem over 35 years after His death.
Acts 13:42-44	Paul both kept the Sabbath himself and met to worship

God with the whole city, Jews and Gentiles alike.

Acts 16:13 — In Philippi, Paul met privately with a group of believers in a country setting, since there was no established Christian church.

Rev. 1:10 — The Lord still has a special day at the end of the first century. *Rev. 1:10* does not clearly reveal which day is the Lord's day, but *Matt. 12:8, Mk. 2:27,28,* and *Lk. 6:5* do.

Matt. 12:8 — The Son of Man is Lord also of the Sabbath. If the Son of Man is Lord of the Sabbath, the Sabbath must be the Lord's day.

Lk. 23:54-56; 24:1 — This passage lists three days in succession.

The day Christ died—the preparation—Friday.

The day Jesus rested in the tomb—Sabbath—Saturday.

The day Jesus resurrected—the first day—Sunday.

The Sabbath is clearly Saturday, the *seventh day of the week.*

Heb. 13:8 — Jesus is the same yesterday, today and forever.

Isa. 66:22,23 — In the new heavens and new earth we shall keep Sabbath each week.

Commonly Asked Questions Regarding the Bible Sabbath

Since Paul declares "Let no one judge you regarding the Bible Sabbath," isn't Sabbath-keeping unnecessary *(Col. 2:16,17)*?

This passage, *Col. 2:16,17* is one of the most misunderstood passages in the Bible. One principle of Bible interpretation is that you do not allow what may be somewhat unclear to keep you from doing what you understand. The Bible is plain on the Sabbath. It was given at creation *(Gen. 2:1-3)*. Jesus observed it *(Lk. 4:16)*. Paul observed it *(Acts 13:42-44)*, and it will be observed in heaven *(Isa. 66:22,23)*. The Bible mentions two kinds of sabbaths. The seventh-day Sabbath and the yearly sabbaths. The seventh-day Sabbath, instituted at creation and part of the Ten Commandment law, is a weekly reminder of the loving, all-powerful Creator. The yearly Sabbath relates specifically to the history of Israel. *Col. 2:16,17* specifically states "Let no one judge you regarding sabbath days which are a shadow of things to come." The seventh-day Sabbath is a memorial of creation not a shadow of something to come. *Heb. 10:1* connects the law of shadows with animal sacrifice. *Ezek. 45:17* uses the exact same expressions in the exact same order as *Col. 2:16,17* and connects it all with the ceremonial systems of feasts and sacrifices (meat offerings, drink offerings, feasts, new moons, and sabbaths to make reconciliation for the house of Israel. *Lev. 23:3* discusses the Seventh-day Sabbath. *Lev. 23:5-32* discusses the ceremonial sabbaths (passover, *verse 5;* unleavened bread, *verse 6;* wave sheaf, *verse 10;* first fruits, *verse 17;* trumpets, *verse 24;* Day of atonement, *verses 27-32;* tabernacles, *verses 34-36)*. Both the feast of trumpets *(verse 24),* and the Day of Atonement *(verse 32)* are specifically called sabbaths.

These annual sabbaths were intimately connected to events foreshadowing Christ's death and His Second Coming. They were designed by God to be shadows or pointers to the coming Messiah. *Lev. 23:37* uses the language of *Col. 2:16,17* to describe these ceremonial sabbaths. *Lev. 23:38* distinguishes the ceremonial sabbaths from the seventh-day Sabbaths by using the expression "Beside the sabbaths of the Lord." Since Christ has come, the shadowy sabbaths of the ceremonial law have found their fulfillment in Him. The seventh-day Sabbath continues to lead us back to the Creator God who made us. God's people will keep it as a distinguishing sign of their relationship to Him *(Rev. 14:12, Ezek. 20:12,20)*.

What about *Rom. 14:5*? "One man esteems one day above another; another esteems every day alike. Let every man be fully persuaded in his own mind." Really, what difference does a day make?

Sometimes it's helpful to carefully notice what a Bible text does not say as well as what it does say. *Verses 5* and *6* say nothing about either worship or the Sabbath. They simply talk about regarding a day. To say this particular day is the Sabbath is an unwarranted assumption. *Rom. 14:1* sets the tone for the entire passage indicating that the discussion focuses on "doubtful disputations" or disputes on doubtful matters. Is the seventh-day Sabbath set apart by God at creation *(Gen. 2:1-3)* placed within the heart of the moral law *(Ex. 20:8-11)* a doubtful matter? Certainly not! The key to our passage is found in *verse 6* which states, "He that regards the day regards it unto the Lord, and he that regardeth not the day regards it not to the Lord. He that eateth, eateth to the Lord for He giveth God thanks, and he that eateth not to the Lord, he eateth not for he giveth God thanks." The issue revolved around fast days not Sabbath days. Some Jewish Christians believed there was particular merit in fasting on certain days. They judged others by their own standards. The Pharisees fasted at least twice a week and boasted about it *(Lk. 18:12)*. In *Rom. 14,* Paul is pointing out that to fast or not to fast on a certain day is a matter of individual conscience, not a matter of God's command.

Didn't the disciples meet on the first day of the week? Acts 20:7

The reason this meeting is mentioned in the narrative is because Paul was leaving the next day and worked a mighty miracle in raising Eutychus from the dead. It is clear that the meeting is a night meeting. It is the dark part of the first day of the week *(Acts 20:7)*. In Bible times, the dark part of the day preceded the light part *(Gen. 1:5)*. The Sabbath was observed from Friday night at sunset to Saturday night at sunset. *(Lev. 23:32, Mk. 1:32)*. If this meeting is on the dark part of the first day of the week, it is in fact a Saturday night meeting. Paul has met with the believers all Sabbath. He will depart the next day, Sunday, so the meeting continues late into Saturday night. The next day, Sunday, Paul travels by foot to Assos, then sailed to Mitylene. The New English Bible reading of *Acts 20:7* also confirms this as a Saturday night meeting, with Paul traveling on Sunday. If Paul considered Sunday sacred in honor of the resurrection, why would he spend the entire day traveling and not worshipping? The record indicates that Paul was a Sabbath keeper (see *Acts 13:42-44; 17:2; 16:12,13; 18:4*).

Can we really tell which day the Seventh-day is?

There are at least four ways which we can tell for certain that Saturday is the Seventh-day:

1. **The Bible** clearly reveals that Jesus was crucified on the preparation day *(Lk. 23:54)*. His closest followers rested as commanded the Sabbath day *(Lk. 24:55,56)* and Jesus rose from the dead the first day *(Lk. 24:1, Mk. 16:9)*. Most Christians recognize Jesus died on Friday the preparation day, He rested the next day and rose the first day— Sunday. The Sabbath is the day between Friday and Sunday or the seventh-day— Saturday.

2. **Language**: In over 140 languages in the world, the word for the Seventh-day which we call Saturday is the word "Sabbath." Language testifies to the Sabbath's preservation through the centuries.

3. **Astronomy**: The leading astronomers in the world testify to the fact that the weekly cycle has never changed. Centers like the Royal Naval Observatory in the U.S. and The Royal Greenwich Observatory in England affirm the fact of a constant weekly cycle.

4. **History**: The Jewish people have kept an accurate record of the Sabbath through the centuries. For over 4,000 years, they have preserved the true Sabbath on Saturday.

I keep Sunday in honor of the resurrection. What's wrong with that? Didn't Jesus rise from the dead on Sunday?

Yes, Jesus certainly rose on Sunday! But He never commanded us to worship in honor of the resurrection. Just as the communion service symbolizes His death *(1 Cor. 11:24,26)* baptism symbolizes His resurrection *(Rom. 6:1-6)*. The symbol of Jesus' resurrection is not worship on the day of the sun adopted into Christianity from pagan Rome's sun worship, but a beautiful ceremony of baptism as a symbol of a new life transformed by the wonder working power of the Holy Spirit. In the watery grave of baptism, the old person symbolically dies and is buried while a new life is resurrected with Christ.

Isn't one day in seven good enough? Why do you put so much emphasis on the Sabbath?

The issue is more than a matter of days. It is a matter of masters. Through a master stroke of deception, Satan has worked through apostate religion to change God's law *(Dan. 7:25)*. He has cast the truth to the ground *(Dan. 8:12)*. He has made a break in God's wall of truth. God calls us to repair the breach by keeping His Sabbath *(Isa. 58:12,13)*. We ought to obey God rather than men *(Acts 5:29)*. To worship on the seventh day is to accept the authority of our creator Lord, who commanded the day be kept *(Ex. 20:8-11)*. To knowingly accept a counterfeit day of worship is to accept an institution initiated and established solely by man in the apostasy. The real question is, then, whose servants are we—God's or man's? *(Rom. 6:16)*. All the celebrations the day before or the day after my birthday do not make these days my birthday. The world's birthday is the Bible Sabbath, the seventh day. It is a memorial to our loving Creator. No other day will do.

First Day Texts

Ex. 31:17,18 The Sabbath is a sign between God and His people forever.

Ezek. 20:12 The Sabbath is a symbol of sanctification.

Heb. 4:4-6,9 The Sabbath symbolizes our rest in Jesus trusting Him for our salvation.

Lk. 23:56 Jesus' closest followers would not embalm His body on the Sabbath. Certainly the Sabbath was not nailed to the cross for His followers kept it after He died.

Lk. 24:1 The disciples visit the tomb to embalm His body on the first day.

Matt. 28:1 The women come to the tomb on the first day.

Mk. 16:2 The women come to the tomb on the first day.

Mk. 16:9 Now Jesus was risen the first day.

Jn. 20:1 Mary visits the tomb while it is yet dark. (Note—the above texts certainly cannot possibly indicate any sacred attachment by the early believers to Sunday since they did not even know at that point that Jesus had risen).

Rom. 6:3-5 The symbol of the resurrection is baptism by immersion, not Sunday worship.

Acts 20:7 In the Saturday night meeting (see the New English

35

Bible) occurring on the dark part of the first day of the week, Paul preaches until midnight. The next day, Sunday, he travels by foot to Troas, then takes a boat too. Certainly, Paul did not sanctify Sunday.

Jn. 20:19

The disciples assemble on the first day of the week not to worship, but because they are afraid of Jews.

1 Cor. 16:2

"By Him" implies by Himself at home. The original language refers to a settling of accounts. The Sabbath has past. It's the first day— a good time at home to finalize bills, settle accounts and set aside an offering for the Lord's work.

Gen. 2:1-3

God blessed the Seventh-day Sabbath at creation.

Rom. 13:10

Our love for God leads us as obedient servants to fulfill or keep the law.

Matt. 5:17

Jesus did not come to destroy but to fulfill the law.

Rom. 8:4

When we come to Him, through His spirit He enables us to keep the law.

An Attempted Change in God's Law

Jn. 17:17	Thy word is truth.
Prov. 23:23	Buy the truth and sell it not.
Heb. 13:8	Jesus Christ the same yesterday, today and forever.
Ps. 89:34	My covenant (law) will I not break.
Ex. 31:18	Commandments written with the finger of God.
Matt. 5:17,18	Jesus came to fulfill not change God's law.
Gen. 2:1-3	Sabbath hallowed, sanctified and blessed in Eden.
Lk. 4:16	Jesus kept the Sabbath.
Acts 13:42-44	Paul kept the Sabbath.
Acts 20:28-31	Apostasy in early Christianity predicted as coming into the church.
Dan. 8:12	Truth cast to the ground.
Dan. 7:25	An attempted change made in God's law.
Isa. 8:16	Seal the law.
Ex. 20:8-11	The Sabbath contains the three elements of heaven's official Royal Seal: God's name, His title, and His territory.
Rev. 7:1-3	God's people will receive the seal of the Sabbath before the end.
Rev. 14:7,12	God's last message calls us to worship the Creator and keep God's commandments.

Sabbath Keeping

Isa. 56:2	God grants a special blessing to those who keep the Sabbath.
Deut. 28:1,2,15	God offers blessing to those who are obedient to His commandments.
Ex. 20:8-11	The Sabbath is a "sanctified" day set apart from all the rest.
Lev. 23:3	The Sabbath is called a "holy convocation" or gathering of God's people. It is a special designated day of worship.
Lk. 4:16	Jesus worshiped each Sabbath, as did Paul *(Acts 18:4)*.
Lev. 23:32	The Sabbath begins at sunset Friday evening and ends at sunset Saturday evening *(Mk. 1:32)*.
Ex. 20:8-10	The Sabbath is not a day for secular work.
Isa. 58:13,14	The Sabbath is a day to delight ourself in the Lord. It is not a day for our own personal pleasure. Such things as sports, secular games, or entertainment are not in harmony with the holiness of the Sabbath.
Neh. 13:15-22	The Sabbath may be defiled by buying, selling, and trivializing the Sabbath by ordinary worldly activities.

Matt. 12:11-13	Jesus illustrated in His life the joy of doing good on the Sabbath.
Mk. 2:23-28	Jesus provided for the physical needs of His disciples on the Sabbath. The Sabbath is an illustration of the God who provides our needs.
Ex. 16:28-30	When some of Israel worked on the Sabbath attempting to gather and prepare manna neglecting to make arrangements on the preparation day, Friday, God openly rebuked them.
Matt. 11:28-30	The divine invitation is to come and find rest in Jesus. Each Sabbath provides us with an opportunity to renew our commitment with our Lord.

* Statements regarding the change of the Bible Sabbath appear on page 119

Faith

Heb. 11:6	Without faith it is impossible to please God.
Rom. 12:3	God gives a measure of faith to every man.
Mk. 11:22-24	If we exercise the faith we have, mountains of difficulty will be removed.
Rom. 10:17	Our faith is increased as we hear God's words.
Heb. 11:1	Faith is the foundation which supports our entire Christian experience.
Heb. 4:2	We are benefited by God's word as we apply it to our lives.
1 Jn. 5:14	Faith is confidence in God which leads us to do His will.
Lk. 5:20	Faith can be seen. It is manifest in action.
Matt. 17:20	Little faith, as a mustard seed, can grow.
Eph. 2:8	We are saved by grace through faith.
Rom. 1:5	Grace leads to the obedience of faith.
Gal. 2:20	The Christian lives by faith.
Heb. 6:12	Through faith we inherit the promises of God.
Jas. 2:17	Faith without works is dead.
1 Jn. 5:4	We overcome the world through faith.

Health

3 Jn. 1:2	God desires that we prosper and be in health.
1 Thess. 5:23	Sanctification includes body, mind, and emotions as well as spiritual faculties.
Rom. 12:1,2	Present your bodies a living sacrifice unto God.
1 Cor. 6:19,20	Your body is the temple of God.
1 Cor. 10:31	Whatever you eat or drink, do all to the glory of God.
Prov. 20:1	Wine is a mocker, strong drink is raging.
Prov. 23:29-32	Do not drink fermented wine. It brings sorrow, woe, and contention. It is deceptive and clouds judgment.
Isa. 5:11	Woe to those who are intoxicated by wine.
Prov. 4:17	Excessive wine leads to violence.
Prov. 31:4,5	Wine is not for kings or princes since it perverts wise judgment.
Rev. 5:10	Since we are kings and priests unto God, we need clear minds.
Gen. 1:29	God's original diet was a vegetarian diet.
Gen. 7:2	Noah understood the difference between clean and unclean animals. Since at the time of the flood, God gave permission to eat the clean animals, they were brought

	by sevens. The unclean scavengers by twos.
Lev. 11:1-12	Clean animals must have a split or divided hoof and chew the cud. Unclean animals are those like pigs that do not have the above features. Clean sea animals must have both fins and scales.
Isa. 66:15-17	Those who rebel against God's dietary standards will not be in the kingdom.
Isa. 65:1-5	God links eating unclean foods to heathen idolatry.
Acts 10:9-16	Peter's sheet with all kinds of unclean animals, including rats, alligators, crocodiles. God says arise and eat. Peter is horrified! What does God mean? *Verse 17* indicates Peter is uncertain
Acts 10:28	Peter explains that the vision applies not to food but to calling Gentiles unclean. In this vision, God breaks the racial barrier. Peter is open to witness now to the Gentiles. The vision deals with the fact that through the cross all barriers between people are removed.
Phil. 4:13	Jesus provides spiritual strength to overcome physical habits.
Heb. 4:15,16	Jesus was tempted like we are. He fasted 40 days and overcame so we, too, can receive His power to overcome.

Commonly Asked Questions Regarding Health

Didn't Jesus say, "It is not what goes into a man but its what goes out which defiles him"? Why put so much emphasis on health? Does it really make much difference?

The passage under consideration is *Mk. 7:18-20*. What issues are involved here? The New Testament plainly declares, "What, know ye not that your body is the temple of the Holy Spirit....glorify God in your body" *(1 Cor. 6:19,20)*. "If any man defile the temple of God, him shall God destroy, for the temple of God is holy, which temple ye are" *(1 Cor. 3:17)*. Whether therefore ye eat or drink, or whatsoever ye do, do all to the glory of God *(1 Cor. 10:31)*. The scriptures are consistent. They don't tell us to carefully consider what we eat and drink in one place, and then that it doesn't matter what we eat or drink in another. Let's summarize *Mk. 7* in its entirety. The Pharisees had very strict laws regarding ceremonial cleanliness. They believed to touch a Gentile (non-Jew) in the market place was defiling. All cooking utensils, such as pots, cups, and plates must be washed thoroughly lest some Gentile touch them, thereby defiling them (see *Mk. 7:1-5)*. The object of discussion in *Mk. 7* was not the Levitical health laws *(Lev. 11)* given by a loving God to preserve the health of His people but the Jewish "tradition of the elders" *(Mk. 7:5)*. The Pharisees believed that to eat with unwashed hands, you absorbed or took in defilement from the Gentiles. The question here is not what you eat, but how you eat. The issue is not a repudiation of the health laws which our Lord Himself gave, but rather a rejection of the idea of ceremonial defilement by touching Gentiles. In this context "nothing from outside you can produce defilement or sin. All sin results in the mind." The Jews rejected God's commandments, to maintain their tradition of exclusiveness *(Mk. 7:9)*. The expression "purging all meats" (K.J.V.) in *verse 19* is better translated "purging all foods." The word is *broma*. No food is ceremonially unclean. No food carries sin within it. Not from without, but from within sin arises *(Mk. 7:21)*. Jesus did not consider unclean animals food. They were scavengers never to be eaten. The issue in *Mk. 7* is not health which comes by eating unclean animals, but ceremonial defilement which comes by touching Gentiles and transferring it through foods into the body.

Didn't the apostle Paul say, "Meat doesn't commend us to God, we are no better or worse if we eat" *(1 Cor. 8:8)*. Didn't he also declare, "Whatever is sold in the market place eat, asking no question for conscience sake *(1 Cor. 10:25)*?

1 Cor. 8:1 provides the background for the answer to these thoughtful questions. Paul introduces the passage by saying, "Now as touching things offered to idols" *(verse 1)* so there will be no misunderstanding he emphasizes it again in *verse 4* "as concerning those things that are offered in sacrifice to idols." In *1 Cor. 10:28*, at the end of the discussion, he speaks of meat "offered in sacrifice to idols." Portions of the meat which were used in idol worship at pagan temples in Corinth were sold in the market places. This led some very strict Jews to become vegetarians *(Rom. 14:2-4)*. The issue at stake here is whether it is morally wrong to eat meat offered to idols. In eating will one be participating in idol worship. Paul's response is idols are nothing at all *(1 Cor. 8:4)*. We are no better or worse if we eat *(1 Cor. 8:8)*. If your liberty is a stumbling block to someone else, offending their weak conscience, don't eat any meat offered to idols *(1 Cor. 8:11-13)*. At stake here is not unclean foods but food offered to idols. Jesus did not come to cleanse pigs. He came to cleanse sinners. Unclean animals which are unhealthful in the Old Testament are still unhealthful in the New. Since our Lord will not withhold from us any good thing *(Ps. 84:11)* unclean animals are not good things.

Aren't the health laws Jewish Old Testament rituals which Christ did away with at the cross?

When Jesus died, He gave His life to redeem mankind. His death did not affect in any way what is healthy and what is not healthy. It only makes sense that if pork, for example, was unhealthy because it was a scavenger before the cross, it is unhealthy because it is a scavenger after the cross. Contrary to popular opinion, the Biblical health laws are not for the Jews alone. When Noah entered the ark, he was instructed to bring the clean animals by sevens and the unclean by twos. Since the clean animals would be eaten due to the shortage of vegetation after the flood, they were brought by sevens. In *Lev. 11*, God distinguishes between clean and unclean animals for all mankind. *Isa. 65:2-5* describes those who have rebelled against God as worshipping idols and eating swine's flesh. The prophet Isaiah reveals that the rebellious will be destroyed as those "eating swines flesh." God knows best. He desires our bodies in good health. He invites us to give up anything which harms His temple.

Since God told Noah, "Every moving thing which liveth shall be meat for you; even as the green herb have I given you all things" *(Gen. 9:3)*, isn't it permissible to eat whatever we want?

We might ask "was God giving Noah permission to eat snakes, rats, alligators, lizards, worms, and cockroaches?" Certainly not! Noah

45

already knew the difference between clean and unclean foods *(Gen. 7:2)*. God was simply making a statement, "Noah, you may now eat flesh foods." The evidence for this is that God clearly forbade unclean animals later in both *Lev. 11* and *Deuteronomy 14*. Since God does not change His moral standards *(Ps.s 89:34)* and since God's character does not change *(Mal. 3:6)*, He did not give permission to Noah to do something He forbade Moses to do. All God's laws including those relating to health were given in love to reduce disease and increase happiness *(Ex. 15:26)*. Many in the scientific community recognize that the health principles of the Bible can significantly assist in reducing both heart disease and cancer. God's ways are best.

Doesn't the Bible say to beware of those who command you to abstain from meat *(1 Tim. 4:3)*?

Our passage describes a group who depart from the Biblical faith in the last days. According to *1 Tim. 4:3*, they teach two twin errors. This group forbids marriage and commands to abstain from meats *(K.J.V.)* or foods (Greek *broma*) which God has created to be received with thanksgiving. The word meat here refers not to animals in particular, but food in general. The same word is used in the Greek version of the Old Testament in *Gen. 1:29*. "Every herb bearing seed which is upon the face of all the earth, and every tree in which is a fruit of a tree yielding seed to you shall it be for "meat" or food." Throughout the centuries, certain ascetics, monks, and priests have declared the world as evil. Both marriage and food are created by God. They are both part of God's good plan for the human race. According to *1 Tim. 4:4,5*, those creatures sanctified by the word of God are good and not to be refused when received with thanksgiving. Paul here is arguing against the fanatism which declares all physical plea-sure as evil. He reveals that God's creation is good. God desires that His creatures heartily enjoy the food He has created for them. The issue here is not clean or unclean foods, but whether food itself is part of the material world and rejected through monastic life. Paul says, NO! God's creation is good.

What difference does it make what we eat and drink, isn't God interested in our spiritual life only?

Human beings are a unit. Whatever affects the physical also affects the mental and spiri-tual faculties. Our physical habits affect the quality of blood which passes through the brain. A poor quality of blood supplied to the brain makes us less capable of comprehending spiritual truth. In *1 Thess. 5:23,* Paul states, "I pray God will sanctify you wholly, body, soul and spirit." In *Rom. 12:1,* he adds, "I beseech you brethren, that you present your bodies a living sacrifice to God." John adds, Jesus desire for all His children, "I wish above all things, that you prosper and be in health even as your soul prospers" *(3 Jn. 2).* God's word declares it does make a difference what we take into our bodies.

What did Paul mean when He in-structed Timothy to take "a little wine for the stomach's sake" *(1 Tim. 5:23)*?

It's obvious that Paul was not advocating social drinking in this passage. He clearly states, "Drink no longer water." (Anyone who has traveled in the Middle East knows the difficulty of getting pure, unpolluted water), but use a little wine for thy stomach's sake and thine often infirmities. Whatever kind of wine Paul was talking about (fermented or unfer-mented), it is exceedingly plain that the pur-pose of his counsel to Timothy was due to his stomach ailments. Paul's counsel relates to a medicinal use, not a social enjoyment. What kind of wine was Paul recommending? Would the apostle encourage the moderate use of a drink which *Prov. 23:31* says "Look not upon the wine when it is red," a drink which brings "woe, sorrow, babbling, and wounds" *(Prov. 23:29)*, a drink which is deceptive *(Prov. 20:1)*, a drink which perverts the judgment causing thine eyes to behold strange women and thine heart to utter strange things *(Prov. 23:32,33)*. Certainly not! The Bible uses the word wine to refer to both an alcoholic fermented beverage as well as unfermented grape juice. According to *Isa. 65:8,* the new wine is found in a cluster and there is blessing in it. This is obviously the unfermented, freshly squeezed juice of the grape. Referring to the communion wine served, Jesus told His disciples that He would not participate in the service again until He "drank it new with them in the Father's kingdom" *(Matt. 26:29)*. The communion wine representing Christ's pure, undefiled Blood must be unfermented since fermentation is a sign of sin. In *1 Tim. 5:23,* Paul encourages Timothy to use a little wine or grape products for his stomach's sake. Unfermented grape juice has healthful properties for the body. Indeed there is blessing in the freshly squeezed juice of the grape.

Jn. 11:11-14	Jesus compares death to sleep. The Bible compares death to sleep over 50 times.
1 Thess. 4:15,16	Those asleep in Jesus rise at His Second Coming.
Jn. 5:28,29	There are two resurrections (life and death).
Gen. 2:7	God created man out of the dust of the ground and breathed into his nostrils the breath of life and man became a living soul. God did not put a soul into man.
Eccl. 12:7	The body returns to the dust and the Spirit returns to God. The Bible does not say the soul returns to God, but the Spirit.
Job 27:3	The Spirit is the same as God's breath of life or His power.
Ps. 146:3,4	When the breath or Spirit returns to God, the thoughts perish.
1 Tim. 6:16	Human beings do not have immortality, only God does.
Rom. 2:7	We seek for immortality. The Bible uses the word soul 1600 times, but never once uses immortal soul.
1Cor.15:51-54	We receive immortality when Jesus comes again.
Ps. 115:17	The dead do not praise God.
Acts 2:34	David did not ascend to heaven at death, but

	awaited the coming of Jesus and the first resurrection.
Ps. 6:5	In the grave there is no remembrance of God.
Eccl. 9:5	The dead do not know anything.
Job 19:25,26	The righteous will be resurrected to see God at the Last day.
Ezek. 18:4	The soul (person) who sins will die!
Rom. 6:23	The wages of sin is death. Death is the absence of life. The gift of God is eternal life.
2 Tim. 4:7,8	The apostle Paul awaited the coming of the Lord for his final reward.
Rev. 22:12	When Jesus comes His reward of eternal life will be with Him.

Commonly Asked Questions Regarding Death

What does Paul mean by the expression "absent from the body and present with the Lord" *(2 Cor. 5:6,8)*?

In *2 Cor. 5:1-11*, Paul contrasts the earthly perishable body subject to sickness, diseases, and death with the glorious, eternal, immortal body which God has prepared for us in the heavens. The expression "absent from the body" means absent from the mortal body with its earthly infirmities. The expression present with the Lord means present in the glorious immortal body received at Jesus second coming. *2 Cor. 5:4* gives us a clue when the apostle longs for "mortality to be swallowed up of life." These words echo the words Paul wrote earlier in *1 Cor. 15:51-54*, "we shall put on incorruption and this mortal must put on immortality." In *2 Cor. 5* as well as *1 Cor. 15,* Paul longs for the immortality bestowed at Jesus' Second Coming (See also *2 Tim. 4:6-8*).

If the dead are asleep, how could the Witch of Endor bring the prophet Samuel back from the dead to speak to King Saul *(1 Sam. 28:15)*?

There are three important facts to observe about this story:

1. God's clear command through the entire Old Testament period was that spiritualists be driven out of the land of Israel and be put to death. The word of God unmasks all spiritualism as the work of demonic, satanic forces (see *Deut. 18:10-15, Isa. 47:13,14*).

2. Saul had already rejected the prophet Samuel's counsel. He had inquired of God and received no answer *(1 Sam. 28:6)*. The specific reason Saul sought out the Witch of

Endor was because he received no answer from the Lord. What Saul saw was not Samuel. Notice carefully the Bible declares the witch saw "gods ascending out of the earth" *verse 13,* and Saul "perceived" he saw Samuel. *(1 Sam. 28:14).* Since the "dead know not anything" *(Eccl. 9:5),* Satan masquerades as the form of dead loved ones imitating both their forms and voices *(Rev. 16:14).*

3. The ultimate result of Saul's visit to the Witch of Endor was not repentance, confession of sin and life but despair, discouragement and death *(1 Sam. 28:16,20,21, 31:3, 4,9,10).* Deceived by Satan, he surrendered his soul to demons.

Doesn't Paul imply that an individual goes directly to heaven at death by stating that he "desires to depart and be with Christ" and "death is gain" *(Phil. 1:21,23)*?

The Bible does not contradict itself. Paul doesn't state one thing in one place and another someplace else. The apostle is clear. At the Second Coming of Jesus, the righteous dead are resurrected to receive their eternal reward *(1 Thess. 4:16,17, 1 Cor. 15:51-54).* In *Phil. 3:20,21* the apostle points out that "our citizenship is in heaven from whence also we look for the Savior the Lord Jesus Christ who shall change our vile body that it might be fashioned like His glorious body." Again his desire is the Second Coming of our Lord. Writing to his friend, Timothy, the apostle declares from this same Roman prison, "I have fought a good fight, I have finished my course, I have kept the faith. Henceforth there is laid up for me a crown of righteousness which the Lord, the righteous judge, shall give me at that day: and not to me only, but unto all them also that love His appearing" *(2 Tim. 4:7,8).* Paul longed for the return of Jesus when he would see his Lord face to face and be ushered into eternity. Yes, death is gain! For the apostle it meant freedom from the pain of a weary body, deliverance from the bondage of a Roman prison, and security from the temptation of Satan. To Paul, death was a sleep with no passage of time. The next event after closing his eyes in the sleep of death was "to depart and be with Christ." Since there is no conscious passage of time from death to the Second Coming, for Paul, death meant closing his eyes in sleep and waking up to be with his Lord.

In the parable of the rich man and Lazarus, the rich man goes immediately to hell and Lazarus to heaven. How do you explain this parable if the dead are sleeping *(Lk. 16:19-31)*?

It's important to notice this is a parable. It is the fifth in a series of parables. (the lost sheep, the lost coin, the lost boy *(Lk. 15),* and the unjust steward *(Lk. 16:1-11).* Parables are designed to teach great moral principles. Each feature of the parable is not to be taken literally. For example, we do not all have wool and four feet like sheep. We are not metal like a silver coin. The question in each parable is what are the great moral lessons. We get in deep trouble if we attempt to take each detail of the parable literally rather than seek the lesson Jesus is trying to teach. Let's assume that the parable of the rich man and Lazarus is a literal story. Do people actually have conversations between heaven and hell? Can those in heaven see people burning in hell? Can they hear their screams? Do souls actually have fingers and tongues as described in the parable? Abraham must have a large bosom to contain all the individuals who go there? To take the parable literally is to create huge problems. Heaven would be a terrible place if we beheld the constant, ever present suffering of our friends. Why did Jesus use this story? What lessons was He trying to teach? The Jews had a common story describing death as passing through a valley of darkness picturing salvation as fleeing to the security of Abraham's bosom and eternal loss going to destruction. Jesus used this story to teach three lessons. First, the Jews believed riches were a sign of God's favor and poverty a sign of His displeasure. In the story, the rich man who the Jews thought was blessed of God ends up in hell and the poor man in heaven. Jesus reversed the expected outcome.

1. Riches gained by greed, dishonesty or oppressing the poor are not a sign of God's favor at all.

2. The parable describes a great gulf fixed. Jesus clearly communicated that there is no second chance after death. The decision made in life determines our eternal destiny.

3. Jesus points out that if the Pharisees rejected the clear teachings of God's word regarding salvation, they would also reject such a mighty, supernatural spectacular miracle as one rising from the dead.

The Jews were always asking Jesus for a sign. He gave them the greatest sign. A short while later, He raised Lazarus from the dead *(Jn. 11:11-14, 43,44)*. As the result, the Jews became threatened and attempted to kill Lazarus *(Jn. 12:10)*. They also became so angry at Jesus—they were so deceived that they plotted to destroy Jesus as well. They had read the Bible with a veil over their eyes. *(2 Cor. 3:14-16)* They had failed to understand that "all the scriptures" testify of Jesus *(Jn. 5:39)*. When Jesus raised Lazarus from the dead, they did not believe. His words in *Lk. 16:31* were prophetic: "If they hear not Moses and the prophets neither will they be persuaded though one rose from the dead." What an appeal! What an urgent warning. Scripture is our final authority. Jesus used a popular Jewish story to illustrate this powerful truth, thus all the Bible harmonizes beautifully.

What does *Rev. 6:9-11* mean when it describes the souls under the alter crying with a loud voice saying "How long, O Lord, holy and true, dost thou not judge and avenge our blood?"

Personification is a common Biblical method of describing situations with symbolic language. After Cain killed Abel, the Lord said to Cain, "the voice of your brother's blood cries to me from the ground"*(Gen. 4:10)*. Was Abel's blood really speaking? No! Not literally. The language communicates God's faithful loving, tender concern for His martyr Abel and Cain's accountability for his sinful act. According to *Heb. 12:24,* "The blood of Jesus speaks better things than that of Abel." It communicates forgiveness, mercy, and redemption. Certainly the blood of Jesus is not literally speaking. The language communicates God's message of redemption. In Rev. 6, God clearly communicates that He has not forgotten His faithful martyrs through the centuries. Their blood symbolically cries out for God to bring justice upon their persecutors and to reward the faithful ones with eternity. In the Bible, the word soul often means "person or people" *(Rom. 13:1, Ezek. 18:4, Acts 27:37)*. It also means life (see *Heb. 13:17, 1 Pet. 4:19, Matt. 10:28)*. Thus *Rev. 6:9* could read, "the lives of those people martyred for Jesus, symbolically like Abel's blood, cry out from the ground for justice." There will be a final judgment and God Himself will set all things right!

Is the soul immortal?

The Bible uses the word "soul" approximately 1600 times and never once uses the expression "immortal soul". The word mortal means subject to death. The word immortal means not subject to death. The Bible expressly states "The soul that sinneth it shall die" *(Ezek. 18:4)*. Jesus declared that both the body and the soul could be destroyed in hell *(Matt. 10:28)*. Immortality is an attribute of Divinity. Only God is naturally immortal *(1 Tim. 6:15,16)*. Satan's first lie in the Garden of Eden was regarding death. The evil one stated that the effect of disobedience was not death but life. He said, "you shall not surely die" *(Gen. 3:4)*. God's word says, "the wages of sin is death" *(Rom. 6:23)*. Death is the absence of life. Sin brings forth not eternal life in hell, but total, absolute, banishment from the presence of God by anni-hilation. The Bible is clear. Man is mortal *(Job 4:17)*. We seek for immortality *(Rom. 2:7)*. The righteous receive immortality as a gift from our Lord at His Second Coming *(1 Cor. 15:51-54)*. Sinners receive their eternal reward as well. "Sin when it is finished, bringeth forth death *(Jas. 1:15)*. The choice then is between eternal life and eternal death.

What does Peter mean when he talks about Christ preaching to the spirits in prison *(1 Pet. 3:19)*?

To understand this text it is necessary to read the entire passage *(1 Pet. 3:18-22)*. *Verse 18* reveals that Jesus the divine Son of God who was put to death for our sins was "made alive" through the power of the Holy Spirit. *Verse 19* makes a transition and declares that it was by this same Holy Spirit that Christ spoke to the spirits in prison. When did he preach to these spirits in prison? Who are the spirits in prison? *Verse 20* tells us! In the days of Noah, the hearts of men and women were only evil continually. They were in bondage to evil spirits. The same Holy Spirit which raised Jesus from literal death appealed to men and women possessed by evil spirits who were spiritually dead in the days of Noah to bring them to spiritual life. The

Spirit of Christ spoke through the prophet preaching the gospel to men and women trapped in spiritual prisons *(1 Pet. 1:10-12)*. The mighty power of the Spirit opens the prison of sin so the captives go free *(Isa. 61:1)*. *1 Pet. 3:21* makes the illustration even clearer. The experience of the flood is likened to baptism. Just as the Holy Spirit raised Jesus from death to life, just as the Holy Spirit led Noah's family into the ark, preserving them from death and leading them to life, so the Holy Spirit works awakening spiritual life, convicting men and women of sin, providing power for a changed life and leading them through the waters of baptism. In Noah's day, the Spirit led men and women from death to life. Today the Spirit delivers men and women from Spiritual prisons leading them from death to life—all because of the mighty power of the resurrected Christ.

What does the Bible teach about re-incarnation?

Re-incarnation is based upon two premises, neither of which are true. First: human beings purify themselves through their own righteous acts. Second: There is an immortal soul which survives bodily death. The Bible teaches that salvation is through faith in Christ.*(Eph. 2:8, Rom. 3:24-31)* Death is a sleep until the glorious resurrection *(1 Thess. 4:15,16, 1 Cor. 15:51,54)*. There is no second chance after death *(Heb. 9:27)*. Now is the time for salvation *(2 Cor. 6:2)*.

Millennium (1000 Years of Peace)

Jn. 14:1-3	Jesus' promise to return.
Acts 1:9-11	This same Jesus which you have seen go into heaven shall so come in like manner.
1 Thess. 4:16,17	The righteous dead will be resurrected and along with the righteous living ascend to meet Jesus in the sky.
Jn. 5:28,29	There will be two resurrections, the resurrection of life and the resurrection of damnation.
2 Thess. 1:8	The wicked will be destroyed when Jesus returns.
Rev. 19:11-21	As conquering King leading the armies of heaven Jesus will redeem His people. The wicked or unrighteous will be destroyed by the brightness of His glory.
Rev. 20:1,2	Satan will be bound for 1000 years.
2 Pet. 2:4	The chains are chains of darkness. Satan is bound on a desolate earth with no one to tempt.
Rev. 20:1	The Greek word for bottomless pit is "without form and void." (See also *Gen. 1:2*.)
Jer. 4:23-27	The earth is desolate (without form and void) with no one inhabiting it.
Jer. 25:33	The slain of the Lord shall not be buried.

Rev. 20:4	The righteous dwell with God in heaven for 1000 years. Sitting on thrones, they participate in Judgment.
1 Cor. 6:2	The saints shall judge the world.
Rev. 20:5	*(First part)* The resurrection of the wicked to receive their final reward occurs after the 1000 years.
Rev. 20:7	Satan is loosed out of his prison to lead the resurrected wicked in a final attack against God.
Rev. 20:9	Satan and his evil hosts are finally, completely destroyed.
Rev. 21:1-3	God creates a beautiful new world.

A Commonly Asked Question Regarding the Millennium

When Jesus returns, won't He establish His kingdom on earth for 1000 years? I have always thought there will be people alive during 1000 years of peace on earth during the millennium.

In *Jn. 14:1-3,* Jesus states that He is preparing a place for us and will come to take us where He is. *1 Thess. 4:16,17* reveals we shall be caught up to meet Him in the sky. *Matt. 16:27* declares that Jesus will come with the glory of the angels to give His eternal rewards. *2 Thess. 1:7,8* adds when Jesus comes with His angels, He shall come in flaming vengeance and destruction upon the wicked. According to *Jer. 25:33,* the slain of the Lord will be from one end of the earth to another with no one to bury them. *Jer. 4:23-27* concludes that "no man" lives on this desolate earth during the 1000 years. *Rev. 20:1,2* adds that Satan is bound by a chain of circumstances in the "bottomless pit" or abyss. The Greek word *abussos* is the same word used in the Greek translation of the Hebrew Old Testament for "without form and void." In *Gen. 1:2,* when God spoke the world into existence, it was without form and void, a darkened, desolate, abyss of nothingness until God immediately separated the dry land, and then created a new world full of life. Again the earth will be reduced to nothingness. Sin will be destroyed. Out of the abyss of the old world, God will create a marvelously beautiful new world *(2 Pet. 3:13, Rev. 21:1-5).*

Heaven

Jn. 14:1-3	Heaven is a real place.
2 Pet. 3:10-13	Our Lord has promised to create a new heavens and a new earth.
Matt. 5:5	The meek shall inherit the earth.
Rev. 21:1-5	The Holy City, New Jerusalem will descend from God out of heaven.
Isa. 45:18	God created this world to be inhabited.
Mic. 4:8	The first or original dominion will be restored to the human race.
Phil. 3:21	God will give us glorious immortal bodies (*1 Cor. 15:51-54*).
Isa. 35:3-6	All physical deformities will be cured. (The eyes of the blind will be opened, the ears of the deaf unstopped and the crippled healed.)
Isa. 65:17	God will create a new heavens and a new earth.
Isa. 65:21-23	"They shall build houses and inhabit them. They shall plant vineyards and eat the fruit of them."
Isa. 65:25	The wolf and lamb shall feed together. God's new kingdom will be one of tranquil peace.
Matt. 8:11	We shall fellowship with Abraham, Isaac, Jacob, and the greatest minds of the ages forever.

Heaven

Rev. 21:3	God Himself shall be with us and be our God.
Rev. 22:3,4	We shall lovingly serve our God forever and enjoy the closest fellowship with Him.
Rev. 21:16,17	God's new city is 12,000 furlongs or 1500 miles square with wall 144 cubits or 216 feet high.
Rev. 21:18-21	This spectacular city has walls whose foundations are magnificent gems, streets of gold and gates of pearl.
Rev. 21:7,8	Lists the entry requirements for the city.
Rev. 22:17	And the Spirit and the Bride say come.

The Destruction of the Wicked

Jer. 31:3	God's character is one of love.
2 Pet. 3:9	God is not willing that any should perish.
Heb. 12:29	Our God is a consuming fire. To sin, wherever found, God is a consuming fire.
Mal. 4:1-3	Sinners will ultimately be burned up or turned to ashes.
Ps. 37:10	The wicked shall not be.
Ps. 37:20	The wicked shall perish, they shall consume away.
Ps. 37:36	The wicked will not be found.
Matt. 25:46	The punishment will be everlasting. Note the text does not say "everlasting punishing". It is a single punishment whose effect lasts forever.
Jude 7	Sodom and Gomorrah are examples of everlasting punishment and eternal fire. These cities lie in ruins today underneath a portion of the Dead Sea.
2 Pet. 2:6	The cities of Sodom and Gomorrah are turned into ashes.
Matt. 3:11,12	The fire cannot be quenched or put out until it completes its work of totally eradicating sin from the universe.
Jer. 17:19-27	Jerusalem was destroyed by an unquenchable fire which

human hands could not put out. It completed its work of totally destroying Jerusalem, yet Jerusalem is not burning today.

Rev. 20:10   The wicked shall be destroyed forever. Forever does not always mean endless existence but is literally translated "until the end of the age."

Ex. 21:6   A slave shall serve his master forever or as long as he lives.

1 Sam. 1:22,28   Hannah presented Samuel before the Lord forever or for as long as he would live.

2 Pet. 2:4   The evil angels and all the wicked are reserved unto judgment. Hell is not burning now.

Rev. 20:9   Fire comes down from God out of heaven and devours the wicked. Tney are completely destroyed.

Ezek. 28:17,18   Satan himself will be consumed to ashes.

Isa. 47:14   The fire will burn itself out and there will not even be a coal to warm at.

Ob. 16   The wicked shall be as they had not been.

2 Pet. 3:12,13   The old world shall be dissolved but God shall create a new heavens and earth.

Commonly Asked Questions Regarding the Destruction of the Wicked

Is Hell a hot spot burning in the center of the earth now?

According to the Bible, the final destruction of the wicked comes at the end of time. The wicked are reserved unto judgement *(2 Pet. 2:4)*. Our God is a consuming fire to sin wherever found *(Heb. 12:29)*. The fires of Hell originate from heaven at the end of time not some hot spot in the earth *(Rev. 20:9)*. The wicked will be totally consumed. They shall be cut off from the earth (see *Prov. 10:25, Ps. 37:10,11,20,34, 38)*. They shall be consumed to ashes *(Mal. 4:1,3)*. This final destruction will occur after the thousand year millennium *(Rev. 20:5)* at the resurrection of damnation *(Jn. 5:28,29)*.

What about the texts which declare the wicked will burn forever (like *Rev. 20:10*)?

Forever in the Bible can be literally translated "until the end of the age" or as long as he shall live. The wicked are consumed, burned up, turned to ashes *(Mal. 4:1,3)*. The old age of sin and death ends. God ushers in a new age. (see *Rev. 21:1-4)*. God creates a new heavens and new earth with no more crying, death, sickness or pain. In the Old Testament, a slave was to serve his master forever *(Ex. 21:6)*. Hannah brought her son Samuel to the temple forever *(1 Sam. 1:22)*. In both these instances the time period was as long as they lived. *1 Sam. 1:28* clearly states, "as long as he lives he shall be lent to the Lord." Jonah even uses the expression "forever" to describe his experience in the belly of the whale (see *Jon. 2:6)*. Forever was a limited, not an unending time. It was as long as the Lord decreed, until the end of the age or as long as Jonah could live in that environment. The punishment of the wicked will be everlasting *(Matt. 25:46)*. They will be consumed. Burned to ashes, they will be gone forever. It is not everlasting "punishing" or a continued state of torment. The idea of an eternally burning hell would make God a cosmic monster, delighting in destroying His creatures. A loving God must blot sin out of the universe or it will destroy the entire planet. Like a cancer surgeon, He must cut out the disease, however painful.

What about the expression "eternal fire?"

Sodom and Gomorrah, two ancient cities, filled with sin were consumed with fire from heaven. The Bible states that they were burned with an eternal fire *(Jude 7)*. They are not burning today. These two cities are in ruins under the Dead Sea. According to *2 Pet. 2:6*, they were turned into ashes. An eternal fire is one whose effects are eternal, one which totally consumes forever.

Doesn't the Bible speak about the fire which cannot "be quenched" *(Mk. 9:43, 48)?*

The fire which cannot be quenched is one which no human hands can put out. It utterly, totally consumes. As a result of the Jews disobedience, Jerusalem was destroyed by Nebuchadnezzar in 586 B.C. The city was burned with an unquenchable fire. You may read the prophecy of this destruction in *Jer. 17:27*. "The fire consuming Jerusalem shall not be quenched." Yet Jerusalem is not burning today. The fire has done a complete work.

The Mark of the Beast

Rev. 13:1,2	A beast rises out of the sea like a lion, bear, leopard, and dragon.
Dan. 7:17	A beast represents a king or kingdom—a ruling power, civil or religious.
Rev. 17:15	The sea represent peoples, nations, or language groups.
Dan. 7:1-9	The lion, bear, leopard, and dragon represent Babylon, Medo-Persia, Greece and Rome.
Rev. 13:2	The dragon or Pagan Rome gives this new power its authority. Papal Rome received its authority from Pagan Rome.
Rev. 13:5	The beast power speaks blasphemy.
Lk. 5:21	If any human being claims he has the power to forgive sins, he commits blasphemy.
Jn. 10:33	The Bible defines blasphemy as man making himself equal to God. The pope has claimed to be God on earth.
Rev. 13:5	The beast power reigns supreme 42 months.
Rev. 12:6,14	The time, time and a half time equal 1260 days or 42 months. During this period, God's people are in the wilderness of hiding.

Ezek. 4:6	I have appointed thee each day for a year.
Num. 14:34	One day for a year *(Gen. 29:27).*
Dan. 7:25	The Papal power which changed God's law would reign supreme for 1260 prophetic days or 1260 literal years. In 538 A.D. the pagan Roman empire granted the pope of Rome civil and religious authority over the empire. Exactly 1260 years later, in 1798 A.D., Berthier, a French General on orders from Napoleon, took the Pope captive.
Rev. 13:18	The number of the beast is the number of a man. His number is 666. In Bible prophecy 6 equals an error or imperfection where 7 equals perfection or completeness. A triple of six equals the great trinity of error: the dragon, the beast, and the false prophet.

Here is Satan's false trinity. The number 666 is closely associated with the most exalted title of the papacy. Vicarius Filii Dei—means Vicar the Son of God.

```
V= 5      F= 0      D= 500
I = 1     I = 1     E= 0
C= 100    L= 50     I = 1
A= 0      I = 1     501
R= 0      I = 1
I = 1      53
U= 5
S = 0
 112
112 + 53 + 501 = 666
```

Dan. 3:1	Nebuchadnezzer establishes a counterfeit image with dimensions of 60 and 6.
Dan. 3:3,4	The entire kingdom is summoned to accept this counterfeit worship.
Dan. 3:14	The central issue in this time of trouble for God's faithful followers is true and false worship.
Rev. 13:13-17	A counterfeit image will be established again, a false standard of truth will be exalted. The central issue will be obedience to God and true versus false worship. An economic boycott, then a death decree will be passed.
Rev. 14:7	Calls us to true worship of the Creator on the Sabbath.
Rev. 14:9-11	Calls us to avoid the counterfeit Sabbath on Sunday.
Rev. 14:12	Calls us to keep God's commandments as a sign of loyalty to Him.
Rom. 6:16	The issue is more than a matter of days, it is a matter of masters. Where is our loyalty?
Mk. 7:9	The issue centers around the commandments of men and the commandments of God.
Jn. 14:15	Jesus invites us to lovingly obey Him.
Ps. 91	He promises to shelter us in the time of trouble.

Commonly Asked Questions Regarding Catholicism

Was Peter the first Pope? What did Jesus mean when He said to Peter, "upon this rock I will build my church" *(Matt. 16:13-19)?*

Cesarea Philippi was a center of Greek philosophy, Roman logic, and Jewish traditional religion. Jesus set Himself against the back drop of the world's great religious and philosophical systems asking, "Who do men say that I am?" After they answered, "John the Baptist, Elijah, Jeremiah," He asks, "Who do you say that I am?" Jesus longed to deepen their faith. He desired to draw out a messianic confession. Peter instantly responds, "You are Christ, the Son of the living God." This thought could be inspired only by the Holy Spirit. Jesus affirms Peter's faith by declaring, "Thou art *Petros* (a moveable stone) but upon this rock (this immovable foundation—that I am the Christ) I will build my church and the gates of hell shall not prevail against it." The church is built upon Jesus Christ. He is the cornerstone rejected by the builders *(1 Pet. 2:4-8)*. Peter clearly understood the rock was Jesus. Paul clarifies the issue in *1 Cor. 10:4* by proclaiming "That rock was Christ." David declares, "Truly my soul waiteth upon God, from Him cometh my salvation. He only is my rock and salvation *(Ps. 62:1,2)*. There is no other foundation *(1 Cor. 3:11)* except Jesus. The gates of hell will never triumph over His church. Peter denied His Lord three times. He attempted to keep Jesus from going to Jerusalem. The courageous disciple misunderstood Jesus' mission. Jesus said, "Get thee behind me Satan" (meaning Satan was influencing him). No, the church was not built upon Peter's weakness, but upon Jesus' strengths. Peter discovered the marvelous truth for himself. Jesus became the source of his strength, the center of his life and the foundation upon which he stood.

What are the "keys of the kingdom" which Jesus gave Peter and the rest of the disciples *(Matt. 16:19)*?

Keys open and shut doors. Jesus said, "I am the door. No man comes to the Father but by me" *(Jn. 14:6)*. There is no other name under heaven whereby men may be saved *(Acts 4:12)*. All the scriptures testify of Jesus *(Jn. 5:39)*. The scribes and Pharisees took away the "key of knowledge" regarding the Messiah *(Lk. 11:52)*. They shut up heaven. The "keys" Jesus gave to Peter were His own words, His teachings, regarding how man and women could have forgiveness for sin, freedom from condemnation, and peace through His shed blood and death on Calvary's cross. A knowledge of Jesus the promised Messiah opens heaven *(Isa. 22:22)*.

Is it possible for Satan to work miracles?

Yes, it is! In *Rev. 13:14,* John describes, "the spirits of demons working miracles." According to *Rev. 16:14,* and *Rev. 19:20*, thousands will receive the mark of the beast because they have accepted Satan's false miracles. Paul warns us in *2 Thess. 2:9-11* that Satan will work with all power, signs, and lying wonders. The apostle gives us a clue why man will be deceived. He says, "They received not the love of the truth." The only safety against deception is knowing Jesus, the author of truth and knowing the truth He authored. *Isa. 8:20* reveals this penetrating insight, "to the law and the testimony if they speak not according to His word, it is because there is no light in them." *Matt. 7:21* describes many coming to Jesus at the end declaring to have worked miracles in His name. Yet the Savior says, "I never knew you (even when in His name they were working miracles)

71

depart from me, ye that work "iniquity." The word iniquity is the same word in *1 Jn. 3:4* when John says, "sin is the transgression of God's law or lawlessness." If miracles lead to a disregard of the laws of health which God has placed in every nerve and tissue in our bodies or if they lead to a disregard of His moral law, the Ten Commandments, the power behind them is not from God.

What does the Bible teach regarding the virgin Mary?

One of the great truths of scripture is Jesus the divine Son of God was born of a virgin. Isaiah the prophet predicted it over 600 years in advance *(Isa. 7:14)*. The angel Gabriel appeared to Joseph to explain the significance of Mary's pregnancy. The angel astonished Joseph by saying, "But thou shalt call His name Jesus for He shall save His people from their sins" *(Matt. 1:21)*. "That which is conceived in her is of the Holy Ghost" *(verse 20)*. Truly Paul was correct when he wrote, "great is the mystery of godliness. God was manifest in the flesh" *(1 Tim. 3:16)*. The Bible does not teach Mary was sinless *(Rom. 3:23)*. It does teach she was a godly, righteous woman. It does not teach she should be worshipped. Worship belongs to God alone *(Rev. 14:7)*. When John fell at the feet of a heavenly angel to worship, the angel emphatically told him not to do it and instructed, "worship God" *(Rev. 19:10)*. The best way we can honor Mary is by following the instructions she gave at the wedding feast of Cana of Galilee. And His mother saith unto them, "Whatever He saith unto you do it" *(Jn. 2:5)*. We honor Mary by being obedient to Jesus.

True Church

Rev. 14:6-12	The message of God's true church in earth's last hour.
Rev. 14:6	*(first part)* God's true church preaches the gospel *(see Eph. 2:8, 1 Jn. 1:7, Jn. 1:12)*.
Rev. 14:6	*(last part)* God's true church is a world wide, international, mission movement *(Matt. 28:19,20, Mk. 16:15)*.
Rev. 14:7	*(first part)* God's true church calls men and women to give glory to God in their lifestyle *(see 1 Cor. 6:19,20; 10:31)*.
Rev. 14:7	*(middle)* God's true church announces "The hour of God's judgment is come *(see Matt. 12:33,37, Acts 24:25, Dan. 7:9-14)*.
Rev. 14:7	*(last part)* God's true church calls all humanity to worship the Creator.
Rev. 4:11	The very basis of worship is the fact that God made us.
Ex. 20:8-11	The symbol of creation is the Sabbath.
Gen. 2:1-3	God's true church leads us back to the Edenic life of keeping God's commandments.
Rev. 14:12	God's true church leads men and women to faith in Jesus and obedience to His law.

Rev. 14:8	God's true church warns against the false doctrines and errors of spiritual Babylon.
Rev. 14:9-11	God's true church teaches the truth about death *(see also Jn. 11:11-14, Eccl. 9:5, Ps. 146:3,4).*
Jn. 10:16	Jesus, the true shepherd,calls men and women to follow Him and become part of His true movement.
Rev. 22:17	The Spirit and Bride say "come." Through His mighty all powerful spirit and His Christ-centered, truth-teaching church, Jesus appeals to us to become part of His people.

Rev. 17:1-5	God's description of a spiritual apostate system compromising the truth.
Dan. 8:12	The truth cast to the ground.
Eph. 5:31-33	The Bride of Jesus represents His church.
Jer. 6:2	The daughter of Zion is like a beautiful woman.
Isa. 51:16	Zion, thou art my people.
Rev. 12:1-3	A beautiful woman appearing in heaven represents the New Testament Christian church.
Rev. 17:1,2	The harlot of Rev. 17 represents the fallen church.
Rev. 17:4	The colors of this fallen, apostate church system are purple and scarlet, the very colors of the Roman church. Her headquarters are situated on the City of Seven Hills or Rome *(verse 9)*.
Rev. 17:5	This apostate system is a revival of Old Testament Babylon.
Gen. 11:9	Babylon represents confusion. Here God confused the languages. Spiritual Babylon represents religious confusion.
Dan. 4:30	Babylon is a man-made system based on human tradition and achievement *(Isa. 45:22)*.

Jer. 51:47	Ancient Babylon filled her temple with idols and so will spiritual Babylon.
Ex. 20:4,5	Thou shalt not make any graven images.
Ezek. 8:14	Woman weeping for Tammuz god of vegetation. Ancestor worship or "saint" worship common in Babylon.
Eccl. 9:5	The dead know not anything.
Ps. 115:17	The dead praise not the Lord.
Ezek. 8:16	Sun worship enters God's temple.
Ezek. 20:12,20	The Sabbath is God's sign.
Rev. 17:12-14	Spiritual Babylon will attempt to unite mankind, setting up an earthly kingdom of God to enforce a common day of worship.
Rev. 18:1	The earth will be lightened with God's glory in time of spiritual crisis.
Rev. 18:2-4	God's final call to come out of Babylon.
1 Jn. 3:4	Sin is the transgression or violation of God's law. God's final call is for His people still in churches breaking His law to leave and become part of His Sabbath-keeping people.
Rev. 14:12	"Here are they which keep the commandments of God" and have the faith of Jesus.

Amos 3:7	God reveals Himself through His prophets.
Num. 12:6	Visions and dreams are one way God communicates His will.
Rev. 12:17	The dragon makes war with the remnant who keep God's commandments and have the testimony of Jesus.
Rev. 19:10	The testimony of Jesus is the gift of prophecy.
Rev. 22:6,9	The angel appearing to John was the angel of prophecy. That same angel appears in the last days.
Eph. 4:8,11-15	One of Jesus' gifts is the gift of prophecy. This gift remains in the church until the end.
1 Cor. 1:4-7	The church waiting for Jesus' coming will come behind in no gift.
1 Jn. 4:1	The Bible invites us to "test the spirits." Each prophetic manifestation must meet the Bible tests of a true prophet *(Matt. 24:5, 11,24)*.

Test of a True Prophet

Deut. 13:1-4	True prophets always lead to obedience to God's will.
Jer. 28:8,9	The prophecies of true prophets, when they are not conditional, always come to pass.
Isa. 8:19,20	To the law and the testimony, if they speak not ac-

cording to this word, there is
no light in them.

Ezek. 7:26   When they disobey the law,
God removes the vision.

1 Jn. 4:1-3   True prophets place emphasis on the centrality of Jesus
Christ.

Dan. 10:17   In vision, a true prophet
does not breathe.

Matt. 7:15-16   The fruits of prophets' lives
reveal their divine creden-
tials.

2 Chron. 20:20   Believe His prophets so
shall ye prosper.

1 Cor. 12:27,28   God places true prophets in
His church keeping His
commandments to guide it
through crises. Just as He
sent John the Baptist to His
people to prepare them for
the first coming of Jesus, He
promises that His last-day
commandment keeping
church would be blessed by
the Gift of Prophecy.

*Seventh-day Adventists believe that the
genuine gift of prophecy was manifest in the
church through the writings of Ellen G.
White. Her writings do not in any way take
the place of the Bible. They are a fulfillment
of Rev. 12:17 which declares the Gift of
Prophecy will be manifest in God's last day
church. Her writings pass the critical Biblical tests of a true prophet.*

Baptism

Matt. 28:19,20	Go ye therefore, and teach all nations, baptizing them in the name of the Father, Son, and Holy Ghost.
Mk. 16:16	He that believes and is baptized shall be saved.
Jn. 3:5	Except a man be born of water and the spirit, he cannot see the Kingdom of God.
Eph. 4:5	One Lord, one faith, one baptism.
Matt. 3:13-17	Jesus was baptized as an adult in Jordan.
Jn. 3:23	Biblical baptism takes much water.
Mk. 1:9,10	Jesus went into and "came up" out of the water. He was fully immersed.
Acts 8:38	Both Philip and the eunuch entered the water. Philip baptized the eunuch by immersion.
Col. 2:12	Buried with Christ through baptism.
Rom. 6:3-6	Baptism, a symbol of the resurrection, represents death and burial of the old life and emergence to new life in Jesus.
Acts 2:38	"Repent and be baptized."
Mk. 16:16	Whoever believes and is baptized shall be saved.
Acts 2:41,42	They that gladly received His word were baptized. They continued steadfastly

	in the apostles' doctrine— instruction (see also *Matt. 28:19,20*).
1 Cor. 12:13	Baptism is into the body or (church) (See also *Acts 2:46,47*).
Matt. 28:19,20	Jesus gave authority to baptize only to His disciples who taught each aspect of truth as He commanded it. He commissioned His disciples teaching all of His commands to baptize. As the Holy Spirit impresses you to be baptized, seek a Sabbath-keeping church teaching all Jesus has commanded.
Acts 22:16	Arise and be baptized and wash away your sins.

Tithe or Christian Stewardship

Deut. 8:18	God grants to each the ability to get wealth.
Ps. 24:1	The earth is the Lord's.
Hag. 2:8	The silver and gold is God's.
Mal. 3:8-11	Will a man rob God? Ye have robbed me in tithes and offerings. Bring all the tithes to the storehouse. Prove me, said God.
Prov 3:9,10	If we honor God first, He will pour out heaven's richest blessings.
Matt. 6:33	Seek ye first the kingdom of God and all things will be added unto you.
Gen. 14:20	"Blessed be the most high God and he gave him tithes of all." Abraham pays tithe to Melchizedek, a type of Jesus.
Lev. 27:32	A tithe equals a tenth.
Matt. 23:23	In discussing tithe, Jesus said, "This ye ought to have done" but He condemned the Pharisees for neglecting mercy, justice, and compassion.
2 Cor. 9:7	God loveth a cheerful giver.
1 Cor. 9:13,14	They which preach the gospel should live of the gospel.
1 Tim. 5:18	The laborer is worthy of his hire.
Prov. 11:24,25	The heart which freely gives will be constantly blessed with more by our Lord.

Deut. 14:22   God's counsel for Christian finance "Thou shalt truly tithe" applies today as in the days of ancient Israel.

Jn. 13:17   If you know these things, happy are you if you do them.

Christian Standards

2 Cor. 5:20	Ambassadors for Christ.
Isa. 62:10	Lift up a standard for the people.
1 Jn. 2:15-17	Love not the world for the world passes away.
Rom. 12:1,2	Don't let the world squeeze you into its mold *(Phillips)*. Be not conformed to the world but be transformed by the renewing of your mind *(K.J.V.)*.
Phil. 4:7,8	Whatsoever is pure, lovely, honest, just, of good report, think on these things.
2 Cor. 3:18	By beholding we become changed.
Ps. 11:5	He who loves violence displeases God.
Ps. 119:37	Turn thou mine eyes from seeing vanity.
Phil. 2:5	Let this mind be in you which was in Christ Jesus.
1 Tim. 2:9,10	Woman dress modestly, and decently, in suitable clothing, refraining from gold, pearls or expensive clothes, but with good works.
1 Pet. 3:2-5	The true ornaments are not outward ornaments, but the adornment of the heart.
Gen. 35:2-4	Jacob at Bethel meets God in revival and commands his household to remove their jewelry and destroy their idols.

Ex. 33:3-6	As the children of Israel enter the promised land they remove their ornaments.
Isa. 3:16-24	God reveals His displeasure when His people artificially adorn themselves and lack character beauty.
Hos. 2:13	Jewelry is associated with idolatry and forgetting God.
Rev. 17:1-5	The false church is pictured by God as being decked out with jewels. She has left her true lover Jesus Christ.
Isa. 61:1-3	Jesus gives to us true beauty. He clothes us with the garments of salvation, granting us the jewels of peace, joy, forgiveness, freedom from condemnation and happiness within (see *Isa. 61:10).*
Jn. 8:29	I do always those things which please Him.
Jn. 13:17	Happiness comes from knowing and doing God's will.
Ps. 40:8	I delight to do thy will, my God!

The Holy Spirit

Jn. 16:7	Jesus declares that the Holy Spirit is a divine person by calling the Spirit "Him," not "it."
Jn. 16:8	The Holy Spirit convicts of sin.
Matt. 28:19,20	The Holy Spirit is part of the Godhead.
Eph. 4:30	The Holy Spirit can be grieved.
Gen. 6:3	The Holy Spirit "strives" with us, leading us to do right.
Rom. 8:26	The Holy Spirit intercedes for us.
Rom. 8:27	The Spirit has a mind.
Rom. 8:16	The Spirit bears witness that we are children of God.
Gal. 5:22-26	The Holy Spirit produces His fruits in our lives.
Ezek. 36:26,27	The Holy Spirit works a transformation of character, giving us a new heart.
Gen. 1:2	The Spirit participated with the Father and Son in creation and He participates in re-creation.
Rom. 8:11	We need not fear death for Jesus, through the power of the Holy Spirit, will resurrect His faithful people.
Jn. 16:13,14	The Holy Spirit guides us into all truth.
Jn. 14:26	The Holy Spirit is God's teacher.

Matt. 12:31,32   To fully reject the convicting, converting, instructing power of the Holy Spirit continually is to everlastingly commit the unpardonable sin.

Rom. 8:14   As we allow the Holy Spirit to lead us, we become sons and daughters of God.

A Commonly Asked Question Regarding the Holy Spirit

What does the Bible teach about tongues?

The following points should be carefully noted when considering the gift of tongues.

1. In *Acts 2*, tongues was a real language used to break the language barrier, communicate the gospel and authenticate truth *(Acts 2:4-8)*.

2. The word "glossalalia" means languages (see *Rev. 14:6*).

3. There are only three mentions of tongues in Acts *(Acts 2,10,19)*. In each instance, people of other language groups are present.

   a. In *Acts 2* tongues are a real language *(verses 8,11)*

   b. In *Acts 10*, Cornelius and his household upon accepting Jesus spoke with tongues. Peter was a Jew, Cornelius was a Greek. Cornelius spoke in a real language which Peter understood. This confirmed in Peter's mind the reality of Cornelius' conversion. *(Acts 11:17* says it was the same gift the disciples received.)

   c. Paul, the international apostle, witnessed tongues in Ephesus *(Acts 19)*. Every time the Bible mentions tongues in Acts there is more than one language group present.

4. The Corinthian church was Paul's problem church. It was often involved in strife and conflict. In Corinth, Paul attempted to control the abuse of the genuine gift. He set forth the following guidelines:

   a. Only one person should speak at a time *(1 Cor. 14:27)*.

    b. There should always be an interpreter *(1 Cor. 14:28).*

    c. At most, two or three should speak in a single service *(1 Cor. 14:27).*

    d. The speaker understands and is in control of what is being said *(1 Cor. 14:32).*

    e. God is not the author of confusion *(1 Cor. 14:33).*

5. Paul's appeal was for intelligent communication *(1 Cor. 14:9, 19).*

6. Since the Holy Spirit interprets our prayers into the language of heaven, interceding for us at God's throne, it is unnecessary to speak a language we do not understand. *(Rom. 8:26)*

7. Since the highest faculty God has given us is our mind, it is dangerous to allow any power to control our mind. The mind is the seat of intelligence. It is with the mind that we worship God. Any form of worship which by passes the mind can become emotional manipulation *(Phil. 2:5).*

8. Tongues is only one of the spiritual gifts. It is not the sign of the infilling of the Holy Spirit—witnessing is *(Acts 1:6-8)*! Not everyone will receive the gift of tongues (real language) to preach the gospel. When it is needed to further God's work, He will give it *(1 Cor. 12:6-11,18,29,30).*

The Bible's Longest and Most Amazing Prophecy

Dan. 7, 8, and 9	The prophecies of Daniel help to unlock the mysteries of Revelation. Daniel shares the details of the judgment.
Dan. 7:9, 10	Where does the judgment take place?
Dan. 8:14	Now that we know there will be a judgment, when will this take place?
Lev. 16:29, 30	The book of Leviticus will help us to understand what the cleansing of the sanctuary means. (Lev. 23:27-29.)
Dan. 8:16, 17, 19	This then is when Daniel's vision literally took place.
Dan. 8:16	Who explained this vision to Daniel?
Dan. 8:27	Why was Gabriel's mission delayed?
Dan. 9:21-23	Gabriel returns to explain Daniel's vision.
Num. 14:34	The key to biblical prophecy is the day for a year principle. (Ezekiel 4:6.)
Dan. 9:25	This is the beginning date for both the 490 years and the 2,300 years.
Luke 3:21, 22	God anointed Jesus of Nazareth with the Holy Spirit and power. (Acts 10:38.)

Dan. 9:27   This text gives you the exact date of Jesus' death.

Matt. 27:51   The veil was torn from top to bottom when Jesus died.

Note: The first portion of the prophecy—or the 70 prophetic weeks pertaining to the Jews—ran out in A.D. 34. The remaining 1810 years concluded in 1844.

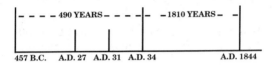

457 B.C.   A.D. 27   A.D. 31   A.D. 34   A.D. 1844

The Time of the Beast: Revelation for Today

Rev. 14:6-12	Jesus reveals His special message to prepare His people for earth's last hour. The gospel goes to all the world.
John 3:16	The gospel is the good news of Christ's saving grace.
Acts 4:12	The gospel reveals that salvation comes only through our loving Lord.
Rev. 14:7	God's theme for mankind is that His judgment HAS come.
Rev. 14:6	God's special message for planet earth.
Rev. 14:7	To what particular time period does this message draw attention?
Matt. 12:36	What did Jesus and the apostle Paul declare regarding the time of judgment?
Acts 24:25	Paul declared that the judgment was yet future in his day.
Rev. 22:11	There will only be two classes when Jesus comes.
Rev. 14:7	Calls us to worship our Creator.
Rev. 14:8	The second angel delivers a solemn announcement.
Rev. 18:4	Calls His people out of Babylon.

Rev. 14:9-11	The third angel's message deals with what warning?
Rev. 14:12	Describes Jesus' faithful followers.
Rev. 19:11-16	Describes the climax of the ages in the return of Christ to deliver His faithful followers.
Rev. 22:14	If, when Jesus comes, His reward is with Him, there must of necessity be a judgment beforehand to determine who receive what.
Dan. 7:7-10	In prophetic vision, Daniel saw this judgment occurring in Heaven.
Rev. 14:17	God's final message of warning to this planet clearly reveals that we are now living in the judgment.
Heb. 4:14-16	Our Lord invites us to find forgiveness and mercy at His throne now so we will be prepared for His final judgment.
Heb. 7:25	Jesus offers to represent us in the judgment.

How to Identify a Cult

Matt. 24:24	Jesus warns us of false teachers and prophets.
John 8:32	Truth in and through Jesus sets us free.
	Identifying feature #1
Ps. 146:3	Cults usually have a single, powerful human leader who becomes the cult's messiah.
Isa. 45:22	Jesus is the sole source of our salvation.
	Identifying feature #2
Mark 7:7	The cult leader's word, or his teachings, become absolute truth.
	Identifying feature #3
Josh. 24:15	Each cult uses "pressure" tactics to coerce its members into submission (Rev. 22:17).
	Identifying feature #4
Rom. 6:23	Each cult denies the central truth of the gospel that Jesus is the divine Son of God (Eph. 2:8).
	Identifying feature #5
1 Cor. 7:13, 14	Cults often urge their "converts" to leave their families (Matt. 10:38; Eph. 5:22, 23).
2 Thess. 2:10-12	Many will be deceived because they did not receive the truth.

John 14:6	Jesus is the Way, the Truth, and the Life. When we discover the way of salvation, He leads us into His truth so we can discover His way of life.
John 12:35	Our only safety is to walk in the light of His Word as He reveals it (Ps. 119:105).

Why So Many Denominations?

1 Tim. 3:16	The apostle Paul defines God's church as the pillar and ground of the truth.
John 17:17	Jesus reveals that His people will be sanctified by His truth in every age.
Rev. 6:1-7	John the Revelator, in the symbolism of the four horsemen, describes the advance of God's truth and Satan's attempt to destroy it.

◆ White Horse—Apostolic purity (Col. 1:16; Rev. 12:1; Rev. 19:7) (A.D. 31 - A.D. 100)

◆ Red Horse—Persecution (A.D. 100 - A.D. 313)

◆ Black Horse—Compromise (A.D. 313 - A.D. 538)

◆ Pale Horse—Spiritual death (A.D. 538 - A.D. 1500)

Dan. 8:12	Predicts God's truth would be "cast to the ground."
2 Thess. 2:3-7	Predicts there would be a falling away or departure from the truth.
Jude 3	Urges us to earnestly contend for the faith delivered to the saints.
Rev. 14:6, 7	Shares the good news that the everlasting gospel would be proclaimed to the ends of the earth.

Rev. 12:17	Describes a people called the "remnant"—those who remain loyal to God, who keep His commandments in the last days.
Rev. 14:12	Describes a people who will keep God's commands and be filled with the faith of Jesus.
Isa. 8:20	Warns us not to accept the teachings of those who lead away from obedience to His Word and His law.

The United States in Bible Prophecy

Bible prophecy discusses those nations which play a role in the overall plan and purpose of God. The prophecies of Daniel and Revelation follow the sequential flow of history, discussing those nations which played a prominent part in God's purposes.

Amos 3:7	God makes the mysteries of the future plain through the Bible prophets.
Rev. 13:1-10	There are six clear identifying marks which reveal that the leopardlike beast of Rev. 13 represents the Roman church: 1). Rev. 13:1—Rises from the sea (Rev. 17:15)—a populated area. 2). Rev. 13:2—Receives the seat of its government from pagan Rome. 3). Rev. 13:5—Claims the privileges and prerogatives of God (Luke 5:20-22). 4). Rev. 13:7—Persecutes the saints (believers). 5). Rev. 13:5—Reigns supreme for 42 prophetic months, or 1,260 days or literal years. 6). Rev. 13:18—The leopardlike beast of Rev. 18 is identified with the mysterious number 666.
Rev. 13:10	The second beast arises at the same time the first beast goes into captivity, or around 1798. It is a separate power.
Rev. 13:11	The second beast rises rap-

	idly from an unpopulated area—the earth.
Rev. 13:11	The second beast has two horns with no crowns. It has no king. It is a democratic/republican form of government.
Rev. 13:11	The beast of Rev. 13:11 is a young beast—or a youthful power full of freedom and innocence—a new nation. (See Dan. 7:17, 23—a beast represents a nation.) In this prophecy, a new nation rapidly rises in or around 1798 in an unpopulated area, without kingly authority, governed by the people. It has the lamblike quality of Jesus, allowing its people freedom of choice. The only nation arising at this time which fits the specifications of the prophecy is the United States.
Rev. 13:11, 12	The features of the lamblike beast rapidly turn into a dragon. Religious liberty is followed by religious oppression.
Rev. 13:12	The second beast (the United States) gives its influence to the first beast, the papacy.
Rev. 13:12	The central issue in the final conflict is worship. (See also Rev. 14:6, 7, 12.) The Sabbath is God's eternal

	sign of true worship. (Rev. 4:11; Exod. 20:8-11; Ezek. 20:12.)
Rev. 13:13, 14	Satan will use miraculous signs and wonders at a time of international crisis to forge a union of church and state which will violently oppose and oppress God's people. (Rev. 10:13; Rev. 19:21.)
Rev. 12:17	God's faithful people will not yield to the coercive pressure to violate God's law.

Practical Christianity

Answers meeting inmost needs

Discovering Truth

1. Approach the Bible with an open mind *(Matt. 11:25)*.

2. Believe that God will reveal truth as you search His word with all of your heart *(Jn. 8:32; Jer. 29:13)*.

3. Continually pray for the guidance of the Holy Spirit. God promises the Spirit will lead us into truth *(Jn. 16:13)*.

4. Attempt to read as many Bible passages on a given subject as possible. Do not build a Bible doctrine on a single text *(Isa. 28:9,10; 1 Cor. 1:13)*.

5. Accept the Bible as God's word revealing truth to you *(2 Pet. 1:21; Jn. 17:17)*.

6. Be willing to make any change from past ways of thinking. You will never know truth unless you are willing to live the truth *(Jn. 7:17)*.

7. Be willing to surrender your own ideas to the truth of God's word *(Prov. 14:12; Jn. 17:17)*.

8. Do not listen to the voice of any counselor who attempts to dissuade you from doing what the Bible clearly teaches *(Prov. 19:27)*.

9. All truth leads us closer to Jesus who is the way, the truth and the life. Seek Jesus in every subject you are studying. Ask, "How can this topic lead me still closer to Jesus" *(Jn. 14:6)*.

Prayer Principles:
How to Really Get Answers

1. Our loving Lord invites us to seek Him *(Lk. 11:13; Matt. 7:11; Ps. 65:2; Mk. 11:23,24)*.

2. Be sure your life is surrendered to His will. Be willing to surrender anything not in harmony with His will *(1 Jn. 5:14,15; Matt. 26:39)*.

3. Bring to Him everything which troubles you or concerns you in any way *(1 Pet. 5:7; Ps. 55:22)*.

4. Mingle praise, gratitude and thanksgiving with all of your prayers *(Phil. 1:4; Col. 3:15-17; 1 Thess. 5:18)*.

5. The purpose of prayer is to lead us into oneness with the mind of God and the deepest fellowship with Him *(Rev. 3:20; Eph. 3:16-19)*.

6. God invites you to find a quiet place to pray and seek Him each day with your whole heart *(Mk. 1:35; Jer. 29:13)*.

7. Learn to pray aloud where only God can hear you. *(Matt. 26:39; Lk. 11:1)*.

8. Record God's answers and rehearse His blessings *(Deut. 8:2; 1 Chron. 16:12)*.

How Can I Become a Christian?

1. Recognize that God loves you with an immense love and desires to save you *(2 Pet. 3:9, 1 Tim. 2:3-5)*.

2. Acknowledge that you are a sinner, lost without Jesus Christ *(Jer. 17:9, Rom. 3:23, 6:23)*.

3. Accept that salvation is a gift offered freely through Jesus. It is not something to be "earned" by righteous deeds or good works *(Eph. 2:8; Rom. 3:24-27)*.

4. Repent of any known sins, confessing them to Jesus *(Acts 3:19, 1 Jn. 1:9)*.

5. Believe that God for Christ's sake has forgiven you. As you surrender your life to Jesus, you are forgiven and accepted. The gift of eternal life is yours by faith *(Eph. 1:4-7, 1 Jn. 5:11-13)*.

6. Since you are now Christ's child, His precious possession, He will begin to work miraculous changes in your life through His Holy Spirit *(Jn. 1:12, 2 Cor. 5:17)*.

7. Our loving Saviour has pledged to guide us from earth to heaven. You may fall but remember He is there to pick you up and get you started on the road to heaven again.

Guidance When Making Decisions

1. God promises wisdom when we ask *(Jas. 1:5)*.

2. Search your heart for any hidden or known sin which may hinder God from answering your prayers *(Ps. 66:18)*.

3. Analyze your motives to discover whether what you desire is for God's glory *(Jas. 4:3)*.

4. Believe not only that God desires to guide you, but believe He will guide you *(Ps. 32:8; Isa. 58:11)*.

5. Discover whether there are any Biblical principles involved in the decision you are going to make. The Bible is a rich source of guidance. God often guides us through His word *(Ps. 119:10,11,105,133)*.

6. Seek counsel from Godly, Christian counselors who believe in God's word *(Prov. 11:14, 15:22)*.

7. Look for providences—divinely ordained circumstances which indicate which way you should go. These "providences" are like sign posts helping us in the process of the decision. They do not take the place of God's word, sound judgment or good common sense. They assist us in the decision-making process *(Prov. 23:26; Eccl. 8:5; Rom. 8:28)*.

8. When you have earnestly prayed about a decision, have consulted God's word, thought carefully about it, sought counsel and watched for providential leadings, make the wisest decision possible believing God Himself is leading you *(Ps. 90:12)*.

How to Increase Your Faith

Faith is trust in God. It is confidence in Him as a well known friend. It grows out of a close relationship with Him in which I know that He cares for me and only desires my best good. The more I know Him, the more I'll trust Him.

1. Faith is the substance of (it stands under, or supports) our religious experience *(Heb. 11:1)*.

2. Jesus invites us to enter into a relationship of trust with our loving heavenly Father *(Mk. 11:22-24)*.

3. Without faith it is impossible to please God *(Heb. 11:6)*.

4. God has given to every Christian a measure of faith *(Rom. 12:3)*.

5. Even a little faith links us with God's marvelous working power *(Lk. 17:5,6)*.

6. Reading the examples of faith in the Bible increases our faith *(Rom. 10:17)*.

7. To receive benefit from reading the Bible, it must be personally applied by faith. Place yourself in every story. Believe God will accomplish miraculous changes in your life as you read His word. Faith grows as we experience it *(Heb. 4:2)*.

8. Expect your faith to grow through a study of His word *(2 Pet. 1:3,4)*.

9. Drawing near Jesus we receive of His faith *(Heb. 10:22)*.

10. To live by faith means a daily, constant, trusting relationship with Jesus *(Rom. 10:17)*.

11. Looking to Jesus, trusting in Jesus, we receive faith from Jesus and our faith grows *(Heb. 12:1,2)*.

12. Faith is not believing God will do whatever we want, it is like Jesus in Gethsemane seeking what the Father wants *(Matt. 26:39)*.

13. We can have the absolute confidence as we sincerely seek His will by faith, He will reveal it *(1 Jn. 5:14)*.

   The life of the Christian is one of constant faith or trust in a loving God who knows best and will always treat His children in ways that are for their ultimate good.

Dealing with Anger,
Bitterness or Resentment

1. Admit you are angry. Be honest with God. Don't try to hide your genuine feelings from Him *(Heb. 4:13; Eph. 4:26)*.

2. Discover why you are angry. God asked Cain, "Why are you wroth (angry)" *(Gen. 4:6)*.

3. Don't let your emotions control you *(Prov. 16:32; Eccl. 7:9; Prov. 14:29)*.

4. Give your anger to God. Remember angry words stir up anger in others *(Prov. 15:1; Ps. 37:7,8)*.

5. Forgive any others who have wronged you. Since God has forgiven you for what you have done to Him, ask Him to give you forgiveness for what others have done to you *(Eph. 4:32; Lk. 11:4; Col. 3:13)*.

6. Forgive yourself for being angry *(1 Jn. 1:9)*.

7. Deal with anger quickly. Don't let it accumulate. If you need to ask someone's forgiveness, do it *(Eph. 4:26)*.

Handling Temptations

1. Satan is the originator of all our temptations *(Jas. 1:12-15; Jn. 8:44)*.

2. God will never allow you to be tempted above what, with His strength, you can bear *(1 Cor. 10:13)*.

3. Jesus faced every temptation common to us, in much greater degree, and overcame *(Heb. 4:15,16)*.

4. Through Jesus' power, the victory over temptation is yours *(1 Jn. 5:4; Rom. 8:5-15; 1 Cor. 1:27-30)*.

5. To maintain victory over temptation, it is necessary to avoid those specific places, pleasures, habits, or things which are the source of the temptation *(Jas. 4:7,8; Phil. 4:7,8)*.

Helping Those With Low Self-esteem

1. A loving creator brought you into existence. When you give your life to Him you are adopted into His family *(Eph. 3:10,19; Jn. 1:12)*.

2. You are unique, one of a kind with no one else like you in the universe. You are special to God *(Isa. 43:1,4,7,21; 13:12; Ex. 33:12)*.

3. Jesus gave His life for you. He wouldn't give His life for a nobody. You have immense value in His sight *(Gal. 2:20)*.

4. Even your physical deformities, inadequacies and deficiencies do not deter His love. All things will ultimately work out for your good *(Rom. 8:28,31-37)*.

5. God has a plan for your life *(Ps. 37:23; Jer. 1:5)*.

6. As you put your life into His hands, He will enable you to fulfill your true potential *(Prov. 3:5,6; Ps. 1:1-3)*.

Facing Fear

1. Secure in His love, you are delivered from fear *(1 Jn. 4:18,19; Ps. 56:3; Prov. 3:23-26)*.

2. It is Satan who inspires fear and God who delivers you from it *(2 Tim. 1:7; Ps. 27:1)*.

3. As you cast your burden of fear upon the Lord, He will sustain you and give you rest *(Ps. 55:22; Matt. 11:26-28)*.

4. His presence banishes fear *(Isa. 41:10; Ps. 61:2)*.

5. Since your trust is in God, you need not fear what man can do to you or say about you *(Ps. 56:11)*.

6. Since He is in control of all circumstances affecting you, you can face them confidently in Him *(Ps. 46:1,2; 91:1-5)*.

Handling Loneliness

1. God revealed Himself to Jacob in his loneliness, assuring him of His care *(Gen. 28:15)*.

2. When Elijah became discouraged, he fled into the darkness of a cave. There, God spoke to him encouraging Him in his despondency *(1 Kings 19:9,11-15)*.

3. God promises never to forsake His children *(Heb. 13:5)*.

4. Since Jesus was despised and rejected of men and left alone to die on the cross, He fully understands your loneliness *(Isa. 53:3,4; 63:3,9)*.

5. When you come to Jesus, He fills your heart with the glory of His own presence. He adopts you as His son or daughter *(2 Cor. 6:16-18)*.

6. When embarrassed and left alone through divorce or widowed by death, a Christian woman has assurance that God Himself will fill the womanly needs of her heart *(Isa. 54:4-8)*.

7. To come out of your loneliness, it becomes essential to invest your life in making others happy. To have friends, you must become a friend to somebody *(Prov. 11:25; 18:24)*.

Overcoming Depression

Depression afflicts thousands in varying degrees. Some depression is so severe it requires medical and psychological assistance to overcome as well as spiritual power. The Biblical principles outlined below will assist you in helping those who are depressed.

Depression Defined: Depression is a sense of despondency in which the present contains little joy, problems seem overwhelming, and the future offers little hope.

You are not alone in your feelings. Great men of faith, Biblical giants, have felt discouraged.

1. Look at David's discouragement for example (See *Ps. 6:6,7; 40:12; 88*). In his discouraging moments, David discovered the following principles for overcoming depression:

   a. God does not forsake us in discouragement *(Ps. 16:8; 139:7-17)*.

   b. Trust and/or faith leads us to rejoice even in difficult times *(Ps. 5;11; 28:7,8)*.

   c. God uses trials and afflictions to draw us closer to Him. In every trial we hear a call to prayer *(Ps. 119:67,71; 62:8)*.

   d. In trying moments, God is in complete control of my life *(Ps. 118:6,8,14,17)*.

2. Praise and thanksgiving in depression is a key to deliverance from depression *(Ps. 118:1; 113:3; 71:1-3,8,24; 59:16)*.

3. God longs for us to turn to Him in depression. He delights in answering our prayers *(Ps. 61:2; Ps. 60:4; 56:3,8,11)*.

4. Unconfessed sin leads to guilt which may lead to depression. If you feel guilty because of some specific sin, follow the biblical coun-

sel *(Ps. 38:17,18* [declare your guilt to God]; *1 Jn. 1:9* [confess your sin]).

5. Pray the prayer of Psalm 51 and believe by faith God forgives you. If you have a general or vague sense of guilt, fill your mind with the thought "God loves me, accepts me, and receives me as His child" *(1 Tim. 2:3-6; 1 Pet. 3:9; Eccl. 1:3-7).*

6. Depression may occur at times for physical reasons. After his mighty triumph over the priests of Baal on Mount Carmel, Elijah became so depressed he desired to die. (Remember this was the man God would translate without seeing death!) Tired, hungry, utterly fatigued by the strain of his stress-filled day, Elijah, under threats from Jezebel, gave in to gloomy, depressing thoughts. Read *1 Kings 19:1-4.* God's answer to Elijah's depression was found in a good night's sleep, a hot meal and words of encouragement. (See *1 Kings 19:5-13.)*

7. While in prison in Rome, Paul discovered the following concepts as an antidote to discouragement:

   a. A sense of God's sovereignty *(Phil. 1:12).*

   b. The desire to magnify Christ in all things *(Phil. 1:20).*

   c. Prayer and thanksgiving in trial *(Phil. 4:6).*

   d. Rejoicing in trial *(Phil. 4:4).*

   e. A sense that God was bigger than his problems and could supply all his needs *(Phil. 4:13,19).*

Healing Childhood Hurts

Many people harbor bitterness against those who have wronged them in childhood. The following Bible study will help those caught in the trap of bitterness to allow the Holy Spirit to heal childhood hurts.

1. The Bible counsels us to put away childish things or hurts from childhood *(1 Cor. 13:11)*.

2. Paul counsels us to forget those things which are behind *(Phil. 3:13)*.

3. We can only forget the past if we are honest with ourselves and others *(Eph. 4:25)*.

4. God knew us before we were born. He has a plan for our lives *(Jer. 1:5)*.

5. Since God is sovereign and we are His workmanship, no one can spoil His plan for our lives *(Eph. 2:10)*.

6. He has a purpose for all that has happened to us and will make all things beautiful in His time *(Eccl. 3:1,11)*.

7. He heals the broken hearted giving us beauty for the ashes of our lives *(Isa. 61:1-3)*.

8. We can honestly forgive others for the way they have treated us because Christ has forgiven us for the way we have treated Him *(Eph. 4:32)*.

9. Extending forgiveness to others who have wronged us lances the boil of bitterness. Just as Jesus forgave those who crucified Him, we can forgive those who have wounded us *(Col. 3;13)*.

The spirit of revenge is self-destructive. As we overcome evil with good, we ourselves are healed *(Rom. 12:19-21)*.

Others may mean us evil but God will accomplish good *(Gen. 50:20)*.

Seven Steps in Helping People Quit Smoking

1. Recognize that smoking is a sin against your body and your God.

   "I beseech you therefore brethren to present your bodies as a living sacrifice unto God which is your reasonable service" (Rom. 12:1).

   "Glorify God with your bodies. Ye are not your own. Ye are bought with a price" (1 Cor. 6:19,20).

2. Acknowledge your weakness and inability to quit on your own. Like the woman with the "issue of blood" in scripture, you may have sought help for years. Or like the man by the Pool of Bethesda for 38 years, you may be desperate in your attempt to stop smoking (see Jn. 5:5-8). Admit that you are weak. Acknowledge you cannot do it on your own. "Without me you can do nothing" (Jn. 15:5).

3. By faith believe that although you are weak, He is strong. Although you cannot do it, He is all powerful. When we choose to surrender our weak, wavering will to His all powerful will, all the power in the universe is at our disposal (Phil. 4:13; 1 Jn. 5:14,15).

4. Surrender yourself and all of your tobacco to God (Josh. 24:15; 2 Cor. 6:2).

5. Believe that victory is yours now and thank God right now for giving you victory over smoking (1 Cor. 15:57; Matt. 7:7; 1 Jn. 5:4).

   You may have a craving to smoke as the result of the physiological effect of nicotine deposited in the cell system. But you need not smoke. Smoking is a choice. There is a difference between the craving and the victory. The victory is yours by faith in Jesus.

6. Destroy *all* of your tobacco. Throw it away. Don't leave any around. Submit yourself unto God and resist the devil *(Jas. 4:7,8)*.

7. Believe that victory is yours now. To sustain the victory, thank God for it! Praise Him you are delivered and follow the physical habits listed below to rid your body of nicotine.

- When you get a craving take slow deep breaths repeatedly until the craving passes.

- Drink 10-12 glasses of water a day for the next five days.

- Relax in a warm *(not hot)* bath before going to bed.

- Plan to get at least eight hours of sleep a night.

- Avoid all coffee and alcohol.

- Take two 30-minute walks each day.

Continually praise God that His power is greater than tobacco *(1 Jn. 4:4)*.

Dealing With Sabbath Work Problems

1. Review the Biblical Sabbath *(Gen. 2:1-3; Ex. 20:8-11; Ezek. 20:12; Lk. 4:16; Acts 13:42-44; Isa. 66:22,23)*. It may not be necessary to read all of these texts. It is essential that the individual is convicted of the Sabbath.

2. Explain that God is interested in the individual's physical needs and promises to supply them *(Matt. 6:33; Phil. 4:19; Ps. 37:23-27)*.

3. There are two significant issues involved in this decision.

   a. Who is my real master? Whose voice shall I listen to *(Rom. 6:16; Acts 5:29)*?

   b. Do I have sufficient confidence in God to believe His word and do what He says *(Mk. 11:23,24)*?

4. When individuals speak to their employers, encourage them to explain that the reason why they want Saturday off, is because of religious reasons. They have recently accepted the seventh-day Sabbath and desire to worship God upon that day. They are convicted based upon God's word that Saturday is the Sabbath of the Commandments and they cannot violate their conscience. They do not want to lose their job. They appreciate their employer, but desire to be off from sundown Friday night to sundown Saturday night. They should explain that they are willing to work any other day of the week, including Sunday, or extra time each day.

5. Present the employer with a written request from the Adventist Church pastor explaining the Bible position. This enables the employer to recognize that the individual is part of a world-wide church with millions of

Sabbath-keeping members who are diligent employees.

6. Bathe the entire process in prayer. Find out the time when the individuals will approach their employer and earnestly pray for God to intercede.

7. Assure the individuals that if they lose their job, God will honor them for their decision by providing for their needs *(Isa. 56:2; 58:13,14).*

Historical Statements on the Change of the Sabbath

1. In response to the question, *"Have you any other way of proving that the church has power to institute festivals of precept?",* Stephen Keenan wrote, "Had she not such power, she could not have done that in which all modern religionists agree with her—she could not have substituted the observance of Sunday the first day of the week, for the observance of Saturday the seventh day, a change for which there is no Scriptural authority."—Stephen Keenan, *A Doctrinal Catechism,* p. 174.

2. "You may read the Bible from Genesis to Revelation and you will not find a single line authorizing the sanctification of Sunday. The Scriptures enforce the religious observance of Saturday, a day which we never sanctify."—Cardinal Gibbons, *Faith of Our Fathers*, p. 111, 112.

3. And Monsignor Segur wrote, "It was the Catholic Church which, by the authority of *Jesus Christ*, has transferred this rest to Sunday in remembrance of the resurrection of our Lord. *Thus the observance of Sunday by the Protestants is an homage they pay, in spite of themselves, to the authority of the*

[Catholic] Church."—Monsignor Segur, *Plain Talk About the Protestantism of Today*, p. 225.

4. "They [the popes] allege the change of the Sabbath into the Lord's day, contrary, as it seemeth, to the Decalogue; and they have no example more in their mouths than the change of the Sabbath. They will needs have the church's power to be very great, because it hath dispensed with a precept of the Decalogue."—Philip Schaff, *The Creeds of Christendom,* vol. 3, p. 64.

5. The Roman Catholic Church cites the Council of Laodicea as the official voice which transferred the "solemnity from Saturday to Sunday." Note the language of one catechism:

"Question— Which is the Sabbath day?

"Answer— Saturday is the Sabbath day.

"Question— Why do we observe Sunday instead of Saturday?

"Answer— We observe Sunday instead of Saturday because the Catholic Church, in the Council of Laodicea (A.D. 336), transferred the solemnity from Saturday to Sunday."—Rev. Peter Geiermann, C. SS. R., *The Convert's Catechism of Catholic Doctrine*, p. 50, 2nd edition, 1910.

Understanding Churches, Denominations, and other Religious Groups

Their origin,
some major doctrinal beliefs,
doctrinal beliefs held in common
with Seventh-day Adventists,
doctrinal misunderstandings, and
suggested methods of approach

Baptists

The Baptist Church is divided into approximately 25 different Baptist bodies with a membership of nearly 30 million in the United States. Baptists trace their roots to the Reformation when certain Bible students discovered the biblical truth of baptism by immersion. Rejecting sprinkling as unbiblical, accepting the literal interpretation of the Bible and salvation only through Jesus' grace, the Baptists grew out of the reformation times. With the Word as their guide, the cross as the center of faith, and water baptism by immersion as the external expression of inner faith, the Baptists carried the torch of truth a step beyond Luther.

John Smyth founded the first Baptist Church in the British Isles in 1611. In England and later in America, the first Baptists believed that salvation is possible for all. They rejected Calvin's view of salvation for a limited pre-destined few. By 1644 there were close to 50 Baptist churches in England. American Baptists trace their heritage to Roger Williams who left the Massachusetts Bay Colony to establish the state of Rhode Island. Strong convictions of separation of church and state led Williams to found a colony in which all could practice religion in harmony with the dictates of their conscience. Throughout the centuries Baptists have been strong promoters of religious freedom. The earliest Baptist churches on American soil, founded by Williams in Providence, Rhode Island in 1639 and by John Clarke in Newport, Rhode Island, in 1648, were bulworks of religious liberty. Baptists have championed two distinct truths through the centuries (1) Baptism by immersion and (2) Religious Liberty. A small group of Baptists have maintained allegiance to the Seventh-day Sabbath. Seventh-day Adventists have much in common with their Baptist brothers and sisters.

Some doctrinal beliefs held in common with Baptists

1. The Bible as the only rule of faith and practice (although some Baptists hold to verbal inspiration of every word of the Bible).

2. Salvation by grace alone.

3. The Godhead.

4. The fact of Jesus Second Coming.

5. Baptism by immersion.

6. Separation of church and state.

Some major doctrinal misunderstandings of Baptists and Bible texts to meet them

1. **The secret rapture:** The belief that Christ will return secretly prior to the tribulation (plagues) to snatch away or rapture His church leaving the unsaved on earth to suffer through the plagues.

   (See *1 Thess. 4:16,17; 2 Thess. 1:7-9; Matt. 13:30; Luke 17: 26-37; Matt. 24:27; Ps. 50:3; Rev. 1:7.*)

2. **Immortality of the soul:** The belief that each individual has an immortal, indestructible soul distinct from the body but which leaves the body at death destined for heaven or hell.

   (See *1 Tim. 6:15,16; Gen. 2:7; Eccl. 12:7; Job 27:3; Ps. 146:4; 6:5; 115:17; Jn. 11:11-14.*) Remember the Bible uses the word "soul" 1,600 times and never *once* says "immortal soul." The Bible calls death a sleep 53 times.

3. **Eternal torment**: The belief that God punishes the lost in hell for eternity.

   (See *Mal. 4:1-3; Ps. 37:10,11,20,38; Jude 7; 2 Pet. 2:6; Rev. 20:9; Heb. 12:29.*)

4. **Once saved always saved:** The belief that once an individual comes to Christ they can never lose their salvation.

   (See *1 Cor. 15:1,2; 2 Pet. 2:20-22; 1 Cor. 9:27* [The word castaway here is the same word used in *Jer. 6:30* for burned or rejected]; *Heb. 4:4-7; Rev. 3:5;* see also *Phil. 4:3*—When we accept Christ, our names are placed in the Book of Life. Since they can be removed, it is possible for those who once accepted to reject.)

5. **Sunday sacredness:** The belief that since Jesus rose from the dead on the first day, all Christians should worship on that day.

   (See *Gen. 2:1-3; Ex. 20:8-11; Ezek. 20:12-20; Luke 4:16; Matt. 24:20; Acts 13:42-44; Rev. 1:10; Matt. 12:8; Lk. 6:5; Isa. 66:22,23.*)

5. **The law was done away in Christ:**

   (See *Matt. 5:17,18; Jn. 14:15; Rom. 6:13,14; 3:28-31; Ps. 40:8; Heb. 8:10; 1 Jn. 2:3-6; Jas. 2:10-17.*)

Approaches for the Baptist Mind

In approaching your Baptist friends, begin with points held in common. Do not immediately enter into a discussion regarding the Bible Sabbath, talk about Jesus. Emphasize that salvation is by grace. Discuss the importance of understanding the basis of justification as God's redemptive act on the cross received by faith. Explain that love always leads to obedience.

(See *Eph 2:8-10; Jas. 1: 10-17; Rom. 3:15-31; 6:14,15, Jn. 14:15.*) It is better to avoid conflict at any cost. You may win an argument but lose a friend. Establish a rapport. Develop friendships based on a common love for Jesus. Pray with and for your Baptist friend. Spend time sharing your personal experience with Jesus. Praise God together for what He is doing in your life. Once this common bond is established, once this mutual love for Jesus is established in both of your hearts, when the time is right, under the guidance of the Holy Spirit, explain the truths unique to Seventh-day Adventists.

Take these steps:

1. Share your personal testimony regarding what Jesus has done for you.

2. Exchange thoughts on the importance of knowing Jesus in a meaningful devotional life.

3. Share an appropriate Christ-centered sermon tape, or a book such as *Desire of Ages* or *Steps to Christ* or a *Signs* article.

4. Invite your Baptist friends to your home for a meal.

5. Share the "Bible Says" lessons at the right time when your friend seems open.

Non-denominational Bible churches grew out of a back-to-the-Bible movement by fundamentalist Christians during the last 50 years in America. Sensing apostasy in the mainline churches, they earnestly desire to return to the essence of New Testament Christianity. These groups are characterized by strong pastors, whose Biblical preaching and charismatic leadership have led to the formation of independent churches with authority in each local congregation. They are not part of any centralized denominational structure. Their doctrines are somewhat similar yet vary in minor points. Generally non-denominational Bible churches are characterized by:

1. A literal interpretation of the Bible.

2. A strong belief in salvation by grace.

3. A futurist interpretation of prophecy with a belief in the rapture.

4. A belief in the immortality of the soul.

5. An acceptance of Sunday as the Lord's day due to Christ's resurrection from the dead on that day.

6. An uncomplicated, Christ-centered worship service with fervent singing, inspiring Biblical preaching and warm, loving fellowship.

7. A belief in once-saved-always-saved.

8. Most believe the law was done away with at the cross.

Some doctrinal beliefs held in common with non-denominational Bible churches

1. A strong emphasis on the Bible.

2. The Trinity/Godhead.

3. Christ-centered preaching.

4. A belief that salvation is by grace alone.

5. A belief in the Second Coming of Jesus.

6. A sense of the general apostasy in Christianity with the earnest desire to return to the faith of the New Testament believers.

7. A willingness to leave main line churches.

Some major doctrinal differences with non-denominational Bible churches and Bible texts to meet them

1. **The secret rapture:** The belief that Christ will return secretly prior to the tribulation (plagues) to snatch away or rapture His church leaving the unsaved on earth to suffer through the plagues.

   (See *1 Thess. 4:16,17; 2 Thess. 1:7-9; Matt. 13:30; Lk. 17: 26-37; Matt. 24:27; Ps. 50:3; Rev. 1:7.*)

2. **Once saved always saved:** The belief that once an individual comes to Christ they can never lose their salvation.

   (See *1 Cor. 15:1,2; 2 Pet. 2:20-22; 1 Cor. 9:27* [The word castaway here is the same word used in *Jer. 6:30* for burned or rejected]; *Heb. 4:4-7; Rev. 3:5;* see also *Phil. 4:3*—When we accept Christ, our names are placed in the Book of Life. Since they can be removed, it is possible for those who once accepted to reject.)

3. **Immortality of the soul:** The belief that each individual has an immortal, indestructible soul distinct from the body but which leaves the body at death destined for heaven or hell.

(See *1 Tim. 6:15,16; Gen. 2:7; Eccl. 12:7; Job 27:3; Ps. 146:4; 6:5; 115:17; Jn. 11:11-14.*) Remember the Bible uses the word "soul" 1,600 times and never *once* says "immortal soul." The Bible calls death a sleep 53 times.

4. **Sunday sacredness:** The belief that since Jesus rose from the dead on the first day, all Christians should worship on that day.

   (See *Gen. 2:1-3; Ex. 20:8-11; Ezek. 20:12,20; Lk. 4:16; Matt. 24:20; Acts 13:42-44; Rev. 1:10; Matt. 12:8; Lk. 6:5; Isa. 66:22,23.*)

5. **The law was done away in Christ:**

   (See *Matt. 5:17,18; Jn. 13:14; Rom. 6:13,14; 3:28-31; Ps. 40:8; Heb. 8:10; 1 Jn. 2:3-6; Jas. 2:10-17.*)

Possible approaches for friends in a non-denominational Bible church

1. Establish a bond of Christian love and fellowship based upon unity in Christ and your belief that the Bible is God's Word.

2. Spend time sharing your personal testimony of salvation through Christ alone.

3. Emphasize the Bible as God's word is the only standard of faith.

4. Discuss the manner of Jesus Second Coming. Present a study showing that the Rapture is not Biblical. This will pave the way for future studies.

5. Present studies on *Dan. 2;* and *Matt. 24,* the manner of Christ's coming early.

6. A study on "Why So Many Denominations?" from *Rev. 14:6-12, Rev. 17* and *18* will be particularly helpful with this group.

Buddhists

Buddha is the title which was given to a young man named Gautama, who was the founder of the Buddhist religion. Buddha means "Fully Enlightened." Buddha lived in the sixth century B.C. or approximately 2,500 years ago. At one time almost one-third of the world's inhabitants were Buddhists. Buddhism is the principal religion of Sri Lanka, central, eastern and south eastern Asia. It teaches that the secret of life is brotherly love. It teaches that selfishness is the heart of the world's woes and can be stamped out by a system known as the "Eight-fold Path" These "eight paths" are:

1. Right beliefs

2. Right efforts

3. Right thinking

4. Right ideals

5. Right works

6. Right deeds

7. Right way of earning a living

8. Right meditation

The secret of life is love. Only love can banish hatred. Love of one's enemies is the jewel of life. The ultimate goal of life is Nirvana, a complete state of peace and love. One of Buddhism's great failures lies in a misunderstanding of the source of this love, the nature of man in his fallen condition, and the redemption which is possible only through Jesus Christ. Buddhists see God as impersonal, Jesus as merely a God-man, salvation as a cosmic consciousness of peace and love with no personal identity and righteousness achieved by good works.

Possible approaches to the Buddhists' mind

1. Sharing the joy, peace, and love Jesus brings into your life.

2. Asking questions such as "what is the source of love? Why do we do bad when we desire to do right? Do good men lie (lying is one of Buddhism's greatest sins)? Would Jesus, a good man, lie about his identity being God? Why do we fail to achieve good when we know what it is? Why do we feel guilty so often? Why is it that something often seems missing in life?

3. Share that the goal of love is a commendable one. Study the origin of evil. The plan of salvation, and redemption only in Jesus.

4. Establish credibility in the Bible by sharing the prophecies of scripture. Prophecies such as *Dan. 2*, Old Testament predictions for the divinity of Christ, and the second coming are particularly fascinating for the Buddhist mind.

Helpful Definitions

Karma– the righteous or evil deeds or activities of the individual.

Nirvana– the ultimate attainment in the reincarnation cycle of nothingness when the individual supposedly becomes one with the universe resulting in a state of peace.

Reincarnation– series of lives, deaths and births determined by one's deeds on a progressive upward or downward scale toward ultimate peace or misery.

Catholics

The Roman Catholic Church attempts to trace its origin to New Testament times believing Peter was the first Pope. Understanding Jesus words "Thou art Peter, and upon this rock I will build my church"...."I give unto thee the keys of the kingdom of heaven"... *(Matt. 16:18,19)* to mean that heaven's divine authority was given to the Pope, the Catholic Church takes the position that the authority of the church is superior to the authority of scripture. The Bible as interpreted by the church and as understood by the priests must be blended with traditions of the church to arrive at truth. The teachings of church councils through the centuries, the encyclicals, and decrees of the Pope provide a basis for truth.

There are approximately 926 million Catholics in the world and 18.5% of the world's population is Catholic. Considering that only 32% of the world's population is Christian, Catholicism is a dominant religio-political world force. Approximately one in four inhabitants of the United States is Catholic (53 million U.S. Catholics). Many are open, seeking Christians longing for the peace and freedom from guilt which only Jesus can give. Thousands long for the certainty of truth which comes only from God's word. Of all religious groups, Catholics are perhaps the most fruitful field for receiving God's truth.

Some doctrinal beliefs held in common with Catholics

1. The Godhead.
2. The Virgin Birth (although not the immaculate conception).
3. The necessity of obeying God.

4. The inspiration of the Bible.

5. The Second Coming of Christ.

6. The importance of prayer.

Some major doctrinal misunderstandings of Catholics and Bible texts to meet them

1. **Papal succession:** The concept that Jesus gave authority to Peter which has been passed down through the centuries to each Pope as the "head" or foundation of the church.

   (See *Eph. 1:22; 4:15; 1 Cor. 10:4; Deut. 32:3,4; Ps. 62:1,3; 1 Pet. 2:7.*)

2. **The sacraments:** The concept that God dispenses grace through the sacraments of baptism, confirmation, confession, holy communion, marriage, holy orders, or extreme unction.

   (Jesus is the channel of God's grace for the world—*Eph. 2:5; Rom. 6:14,15; 3:25-31.*)

3. **Purgatory:** The belief that individuals not good enough to be worthy of heaven but not evil enough to deserve hell, suffer in an intermediary state until their sins are purged. This concept is based on the false understanding of the immortality of the soul as well as how individuals are saved.

   (See *Ps. 6:5,115:17; Eccl. 9:5; Jn. 11:11-14* as well as *Heb. 4:15; Eph 2:8; Rom. 3:25-26.*)

4. **Tradition is above the Bible:** The understanding that scripture must be interpreted by the church and placed along side the decrees of church councils to be rightly understood.

   (See *Jn. 17:17; 2 Tim. 3:16; Jn. 5:39; 2 Tim. 2:15; Jn. 16:7-13.*)

5. **Immaculate conception:** The idea that Jesus was sinless because Mary was miraculously protected from sin by the Holy Spirit.
(See *Rom. 3:23; 3:9-12; Isa. 64:6; Jer. 17:9.)*

6. **Confession:** The belief that an earthy priest is the mediator between God and man.
(See *1 Tim. 2:5; Heb. 4:14-16; 1 Jn. 1:9)*

7. **Miracles/visions/signs/wonders:** The belief that miraculous signs authenticate, confirm, and establish truth. The Biblical position is that since Satan can counterfeit miraculous signs, all signs must be tested by God's Word.
(See *Rev. 16:13,14; 19:20; Matt. 7:21-23; 24:24; Deut. 13:1-3; Isa. 8:20; Lk. 16:31.)*

8. **Immortality of the soul:** The belief that each individual has an immortal, indestructible soul distinct from the body but which leaves the body at death destined for heaven or hell.
(See *1 Tim. 6:15,16; Gen. 2:7; Eccl. 12:7; Job 27:3; Ps. 146:4; 6:5; 115:17; Jn. 11:11-14.)* Remember the Bible uses the word "soul" 1,600 times and never *once* says "immortal soul." The Bible calls death a sleep 53 times.

9. **Sunday sacredness:** The belief that since Jesus rose from the dead on the first day, all Christians should worship on that day.
(See *Gen. 2:1-3; Ex. 20:8-11; Ezek. 20:12,20; Lk. 4:16; Matt. 24:20; Acts 13:42-44; Rev. 1:10; Matt. 12:8; Lk. 6:5; Isa. 66:22,23.)*

10. **Prayers for the dead:** The belief that my prayers make a difference with God in relieving suffering souls from the bondage of purgatory.

(See *Eccl. 9:5; Ps. 115:17; 6:5; 146:3,4; Jn. 11:11-14; Ezek.. 14:14,20; Ps. 49:7,8; 1 Tim. 2:6.*)

11. **Infant Baptism:** Babies are baptized for the sins of Adam (called original sin). (See *Mk. 16:16; Acts 2:38-42; Matt. 28:18-20.*)

Approaches for the Catholic mind

As with all individuals, sharing in the context of loving friendship, honestly, openly from God's word has a powerful effect. Please keep these points in mind.

1. Catholics generally have a great reverence for God's word although most are ignorant of its teachings, having never studied it. There is a growing group of evangelical Catholics who regularly study God's word.

2. Catholics often go through great inner spiritual conflicts over the issue of salvation by works. They need the assurance of salvation in Christ. *(1 Jn. 5:11-17)*

3. Catholics are often open to a deeper understanding of Bible truth, particularly the prophecies. They are fascinated with such subjects as *Dan. 2, Matt. 24,* and Christ's life predicted in advance.

4. Begin your discussions by establishing the authority of the Bible, follow with prophetic discussions, then lead to how we are saved. Keep subjects on law, Sabbath and change until you have had a minimum of ten previous studies.

5. When you present the Sabbath, give strong emphasis to the fact that it is part of the commandments which all Catholics accept and it is the center of God's law.

6. Gently guide your Catholic friends to understand that the Bible, not the church, is the

basis for all doctrine and the foundation of all moral decisions.

7. Catholics will greatly appreciate your praying warm, fervent, heartfelt prayers in their behalf.

Catholics are often eager students of the word. Their hearts burn for a greater understanding of truth. They long to know God's will. If the truth is lovingly and logically presented, thousands will accept it.

Christian Science originated in Boston, Massachusetts resulting from the purported visions of Mary Baker Eddy in the mid-1800's. The dominant theme of Christian Science is the power of the spiritual mind to control the material forces. They believe the Bible is symbolic and highly figurative. The devil does not exist. Evil is only a figment of the imagination. Sickness, suffering, pain and death are really illusions. In 1875 Mary Baker Eddy published her book *Science and Health* with a key to the scriptures. She reasons that since God is good, infinite and omnipotent, evil is inconsistent with the character of God. Christian Scientists believe *Gen. 1* reveals creation as spiritual and perfect while *Gen. 2* is an allegorical account of the false material creation and the evil results which follow accepting a misconception of man. The church has no ordained ministers. It publishes the internationally renowned *Christian Science Monitor* daily newspaper with a circulation world wide.

Some doctrinal truths held in common with Christian Scientists

1. God is the eternal, loving, all-knowing Father of mankind.

2. The mind has a powerful influence over the body.

3. God still guides His church through the Gift of Prophecy.

Some major doctrinal misunderstandings of Christian Scientists and Bible texts to meet them

1. **The Bible is allegorical:** The belief that none of the Bible's statements are to be taken literally.

   (See *2 Tim. 3:16; 2 Pet. 1:21; Jn. 17:17; Rev. 21:5; Jn. 5:39.*)

2. **No devil:** The belief that the devil is only an imaginary, fictional character.

   (See *Ezek. 28:12-15; Isa. 14:12-14; Rev. 12:7-9; Matt. 4:1-6; 1 Pet. 5:8; Eph 6:10-12.*)

3. **Immortality of the soul:** The belief that each individual has an immortal, indestructible soul distinct from the body but which leaves the body at death destined for heaven or hell.

   (See *1 Tim. 6:15,16; Gen. 2:7; Eccl. 12:7; Job 27:3; Ps. 146:4; 6:5; 115:17; Jn. 11:11-14.*) Remember the Bible uses the word "soul" 1,600 times and never *once* says "immortal soul." The Bible calls death a sleep 53 times.

Possible approaches for Christian Scientists

With its emphasis on positive thinking, wholesome mental attitudes, cheerfulness, unselfishness, and gratitude, Christian Science has attracted a significant number of well-educated financially prosperous members. Church services consist of reading from the Bible, testimonies from believers and homilies from Mary Baker Eddy's writings. Develop cordial relationships by inviting Christian Scientist neighbors to dinner. Sharing books like *Desire of Ages* develop close cordial relationships. The following suggestions may prove helpful in reaching your Christian Scientist neighbors:

1. Establish confidence in the Bible through archaeology and the prophecies.

2. Spend time on legal aspects of the great controversy showing that the wages of sin is death *(Rom. 6:23)*.

3. Be sure to clearly define sin *(1 Jn. 3:4)*.

4. Thoroughly study the plan of salvation and why Jesus had to die.

You will find your Christian Scientist friends extremely courteous and delightful to spend time with. Their great need is to fully grasp the plan of salvation, the meaning of Christ's atonement, why Jesus had to die, and especially what this means personally.

Churches of Christ

Founded by Alexander Campbell in the mid-1840's, the Churches of Christ grew out of the Presbyterian Church. Campbell came to deplore human creeds and systems. During the early 1900's the Campellites split over the issue of instrumental music and the establishment of a Christian Missionary Society. By 1906 the name Churches of Christ was adopted. The membership of the Churches of Christ stands somewhere around 2.7 million today although the figures are difficult to verify since each local congregation is an independent body and is totally self-governing functioning as a unit on its own. The major Beliefs of the Churches of Christ include:

1. The inspiration of the Bible, but they regard the Old Testament as inferior to the New Testament. They believe that all forms of worship, organization, doctrine, discipline, church administration and fundamental beliefs must come from the New Testament alone.

2. We are under the New Covenant and all Old Testament requirements are done away (Sabbath, healthful living etc.)

3. Immortality of the soul and eternal torment.

4. Sunday sacredness, arguing that Sunday is not the old covenant Sabbath but the new covenant Lord's day.

5. Communion must be celebrated at every worship service.

6. They believe the name "Church of Christ" is the only Biblically true name for a church. They use such texts as *Rom. 16:16; Col. 1:24; Eph. 5:27*.

Some doctrinal beliefs held in common with Churches of Christ

1. The importance of the Bible as the foundation of faith.

2. Christ as the only Savior of mankind.

3. The literal, visible, audible Second Coming of Jesus.

4. Baptism by immersion.

5. Witnessing is a way of life for each believer.

Some major doctrinal misunderstandings of Churches of Christ and Bible texts to meet them

1. **The Old Testament is somewhat inferior to the New Testament.** All doctrine must come from the New Testament alone.

   (See *2 Tim. 3:16,17; 2 Pet. 1:21; 1 Pet. 1:9-11; Lk. 24:27,44.*)

2. **Sunday sacredness:** The belief that since Jesus rose from the dead on the first day, all Christians should worship on that day.

   (See *Gen. 2:1-3; Ex. 20:8-11; Ezek. 20:12-20; Lk. 4:16; Matt. 24:20; Acts 13:42-44; Rev. 1:10; Matt. 12:8; Lk. 6:5; Isa. 66:22,23.)*

3. **Immortality of the soul:** The belief that each individual has an immortal, indestructible soul distinct from the body but which leaves the body at death destined for heaven or hell.

   (See *1 Tim. 6:15,16; Gen. 2:7; Eccl. 12:7; Job 27:3; Ps. 146:4; 6:5; 115:17; Jn. 11:11-14.)* Remember the Bible uses the word "soul" 1,600 times and never *once* says "immortal soul." The Bible calls death a sleep 53 times.

4. **Eternal torment**: The belief that God punishes the lost in hell for eternity.

(See *Mal. 4:1-3; Ps. 37:10,11,20,38; Jude 7; 2 Pet. 2:6; Rev. 20:9; Heb. 12:29.*)

5. **The name Church of Christ** is divinely inspired and chosen of God as the name of the New Testament church.

   (See *Matt. 7:21-27; 1 Jn. 2:3,4; Rev. 14:12; Jn. 14:15; 15:14.*)

6. **The New Covenant does away with God's law**.

   (See *Heb. 8:10; Jn. 14:15; Jas. 2:10-12; 1 Jn. 2:3,4; Rev. 14:12.*)

7. **We are currently living in the "dispensation" of the "church age"** in which God deals with us primarily giving instruction through Paul's epistles.

   (See *Jn. 5:34; 2 Tim. 3:16,17; Jer. 15:16; Jn. 6:63; Lk. 24:27,44.*) Jesus and His Word are the example for the Christian *(Matt. 7:21-27; Isa. 8:20; Ps. 119:105).*

Possible approaches for members of the Church of Christ

1. Develop a strong bond of friendship. Often they are quite argumentive. They really attempt to press the argument of the name Church of Christ as well as the idea that we are under the New Covenant.

2. It is better to share your personal testimony of Jesus first. Avoid argument if at all possible.

3. Share literature like *Signs of the Times* articles on the return of our Lord. The book *Open Secrets* by Don and Marge Gray might be helpful. *Steps to Christ* is excellent!

4. As you notice an openness or receptivity begin a series of studies on the prophecies of Daniel and Revelation. The prophetic messages will stimulate their thinking into the deeper truths of Scripture.

5. Establish weekly contact with *The Bible Says* lessons or invite them to a series of evangelistic meetings.

Episcopalians

Episcopalians trace their roots to English Anglicanism when Henry VIII separated from the Roman Catholic Church in 1534 for political reasons. The Episcopal Church has retained a Catholic style liturgy with the archbishops, bishops, and priests. Episcopalians accept the scriptures as pastoral, filled with instruction for Christian living rather than dogmatic statements of authoritative doctrine. There are no rigid rules. Scripture is accepted as interpreted by tradition. The church is extremely tolerant, permissive, and very socially active. As such it is strongly ecumenical. There are approximately 2.5 million Episcopalians in the United States. The *Book of Common Prayer* issued in 1549 provides a basis for their doctrinal beliefs. Their creed retains infant baptism, the immortality of the soul, Sunday worship, and a view that the Bible is culturally conditioned. They see the Bible as containing God's word not being the authoritative word of God normative for Christian doctrine. Some question the Virgin Birth, the divinity of Christ, miracles, a literal Second Coming, and the reality of angels.

Some doctrinal beliefs held in common with Episcopalians

1. The Godhead—the existence of three co-equal, co-eternal loving, all-powerful, all knowing separate distinct beings—the Father, the Son, and the Holy Spirit.

2. The nature of God—Episcopalians and Seventh-day Adventists both strongly emphasize the fact that God is love.

3. The ultimate triumph of truth—Episcopalians and Seventh-day Adventists both be-

lieve in the final analysis God's purposes will be accomplished.

4. Prayer—Episcopalians and Seventh-day Adventists both believe in a God who answers prayer.

5. Social conscience—Both Episcopalians and Seventh-day Adventists believe that Christian love leads to caring for poor, suffering humanity through social involvement.

Some major doctrinal misunderstanding of Episcopalians and Bible texts to meet them

1. **The Bible is culturally conditioned so not authoritative for faith**

   (See *2 Tim. 3:16,17; Jn. 17:17; 2 Pet. 1:21; 1 Tim. 2:15; Jn. 7:17*).

2. **Sunday sacredness:** The belief that since Jesus rose from the dead on the first day, all Christians should worship on that day.

   (See *Gen. 2:1-3; Ex. 20:8-11; Ezek. 20:12,20; Lk. 4:16; Matt. 24:20; Acts 13:42-44; Rev. 1:10; Matt. 12:8; Lk. 6:5; Isa. 66:22,23.*)

3. **Immortality of the soul:** The belief that each individual has an immortal, indestructible soul distinct from the body but which leaves the body at death destined for heaven or hell.

   (See *1 Tim. 6:15,16; Gen. 2:7; Eccl. 12:7; Job 27:3; Ps. 146:4; 6:5; 115:17; Jn. 11:11-14.*) Remember the Bible uses the word "soul" 1,600 times and never *once* says "immortal soul." The Bible calls death a sleep 53 times.

4. **Infant Baptism:** Babies are baptized for the sins of Adam (called original sin).

   (See *Matt. 3:13-17; Col. 2:12; Matt. 28:19,20; Rom. 6:1-6; Acts 8:35-38; Acts 2:38-41; Mk. 16:15,16; Jn. 3:23*)

5. **Salvation comes by living a good moral life**.

   (See *Rom. 3:10; Jer. 17:9; Isa. 64:6; 2 Cor. 5:21; Gal. 3:13; Rom. 3:23-28; 5:18*) Present clearly to your Episcopal friends the beauty of Christ's sacrifice.

Possible approaches to Episcopal friends

Episcopalians are generally extremely friendly, caring, loving people. As you develop personal relationships with your Episcopalian friends, openly share your testimony. Describe what Jesus means to you. Remember that the love of Jesus will melt hearts when the mere reiteration of doctrine will accomplish nothing. As interest develops through your testimony share a study on the inspiration of the Bible. This is essential due to the extremely loose Episcopalian view of scripture. Follow with clearly prophetic studies such as *Dan. 2, Matt. 24*, and the manner of Christ's coming. The Spirit will touch hearts. Many will awaken to new life in Christ from their spiritual slumber.

Hindus

The Hindus derive their name from *Hindustan*, a Persian word meaning the land of the Indus or Hindus. Often this name was applied to the whole Peninsula of India. Hindu men are often distinguished by their long, flowing turbans while Hindu women are characterized by their colorful saris. Traditionally, the Hindus' have been divided into four casts: the Brahmins, the Kshatriyas, the Vaishyas and the Shudras. Members of no cast were called "the untouchables!" Tribal fighting between castes is quite common. The Brahman cast is considered the highest, most intelligent and superior cast. Inter-marriage between casts, close association with members of other casts, business partnerships between members of varying casts are all forbidden.

Hindu's generally believe:

1. God is an impersonal being present everywhere. Consequently they are pantheists.

2. Ultimate salvation comes through purification via righteous deeds or works.

3. Re-incarnation or a series of deaths and births until one has fulfilled the cycle of perfection called *Karma*.

4. Jesus was merely a good man, and enlightened teacher, or prophet.

5. The ancient Indian scriptures such as the *Bagda Vita* are of superior quality to the moral teachings of the Bible.

6. The essence of life is to develop the "god within" to a state of moral perfection.

Possible Approaches

There is very little similarity between Christianity and Hinduism. Common ground is minimal. Most approaches by Christians to reach Hindus' have not been successful. Since they do not accept the Bible, there is little basis for beginning except friendship and philosophical reasoning. We suggest the following:

1. Establish a personal friendship. Invite Hindu friends for dinner. They will appreciate a vegetarian meal. This is one point of contact.

2. Discuss the concept of good and evil. Ask where did the evil come from and why?

3. Attempt to reason that if God's creation is personal, intelligent, and rational, God must be a personal, intelligent, loving being. If He is not a personal, intelligent, loving being, how could something impersonal create someone personal? How could the non-intelligent produce the intelligent? How could something non-loving produce someone loving? Ask, "Where does the source of love originate?" Discuss Hindu castes, asking why, if we are all God's children, is there so much fighting and killing between castes.

4. After a few visits, share a study on the Inspiration of the Bible.

5. Proceed with your personal testimony regarding Jesus.

6. Carefully review the plan of salvation.

7. Re-incarnation is not Biblical for the following reasons:

   a. Salvation comes through Jesus not good works *(Eph. 2:8-10; 2 Cor. 5:21)*.

   b. Human nature is fallen, we are not exalted gods *(Jer. 17:9; Isa. 54:6)*.

   c. There is no second chance after death *(Heb. 9:27,28; 2 Cor. 6:2)*.

   d. The soul is not immortal *(Eccl. 9:5; Ps. 115:17; Jn. 11:11-14)*.

Hindus are generally quite tolerant with Christians, particularly those living in a Christian culture. Hindus living in the United States or Western Europe will be much easier to reach with the gospel than Hindus living in India. The gospel is trans-cultural. It penetrates the hearts of men and women everywhere. It brings relief from oppressive burdens, deliverance from the pangs of a guilty conscience, and assurance in Christ. Share your personal testimony with your Hindu friends and watch the Holy Spirit work.

Islam (Muslims)

The Muslim religion is one of the fastest growing world religious. Its global scope embraces more than 800 million adherents. Established by Mohammed in the early seventh century, the Muslim faith emphasizes total obedience to the one God, Allah (the God of the Bible). The word Islam comes from a root word meaning surrender, submitting oneself to God, renouncing any other object of worship. The idea of peace is associated with the Arabic root *salam*. The primary religious duties of Islam are five:

1. To pronounce *Shahada* or testimony "There is no God but Allah, and Mohammed is the apostle of God."

2. The ritual prayer *(Salat)* performed five times a day (dawn, noon, afternoon, sundown, and evening) facing Mohammed's birthplace, Mecca.

3. Almsgiving *(Zakat)* or a fixed percentage tax levied by Muslim governments upon the faithful.

4. A fast during the month of Ramadan.

5. *Hajj* or a pilgrimage to Mecca at least once in a lifetime.

Muslims accept the *Koran* as the verbatim, unadulterated, direct speech or language of God. They trace their origin to Abraham whom they believe offered up Ishmael as the child of promise rather than Isaac. Tracing their lineage through Abraham, Moses, and John the Baptist, they believe Jesus simply to be a prophet. Islam is closer to Judaism and Christianity than any of the other great world religions. The Muslims claim Judiasm failed and Christianity became spiritually corrupt, therefore God raised up the prophet

149

Mohammed to reform the corruptions of an apostate religion.

Some doctrinal beliefs held in common with Muslims

1. Muslims believe in an almighty, all-knowing, loving God.

2. Muslims believe in the final judgment. They accept the fact that human beings are morally responsible for their actions.

3. Muslims believe in a final resurrection from the dead at the Messiah's return.

4. Muslims give great emphasis to assisting and helping the poor.

5. Muslims place priority on prayer.

6. Muslims forbid alcohol, gambling, and pork.

7. Muslims place emphasis on obedience to God.

8. Muslims believe in a great controversy between good and evil.

Some Muslim beliefs contrary to Biblical thought and Bible texts to meet them

1. **Jesus is a prophet but not the eternal Son of God.**

   (See *Jn. 8:58* compare with *Ex. 3:14; Heb. 1:6-8; Mic. 5:2; Isa. 9:6.*)

2. **The Bible is not really reliable** since it is filled with human error and has not been copied accurately.

   (See *2 Tim. 3:16; 2 Pet. 1:21; Ps. 12: 6;7; Matt. 24:35; Ps. 119:105.*)

3. **Salvation is attained by following the five religious duties of Islam.**

   (See *Rom. 3:23; Isa. 59:1,2; Rom. 6:23; Eph. 2:8; Heb. 2:8,9; 2 Cor. 5:21; Gal. 3:13.*)

4. **Revelations through Mohammed supersede the Bible.** They provide a source of salvation.

   (See *Jn. 17:17; 14:6; Acts 4:12; Isa. 45:22.*)

Possible approaches to Muslim friends

1. Develop a friendship based on the points we hold in common.

2. Invite your Muslim friends to your home for a vegetarian meal.

3. Share your concern for genuine Christianity. Acknowledge the apostasy in Christianity and the need for reform.

4. Studies on Biblical prophecy help to confirm the authenticity of the scriptures.

5. Since the Muslim family unit is extremely strong with the father's leadership role highly respected, be sure to respect the Father as the family leader.

6. Share literature such as *Prophets and Kings* as well as *Patriarchs and Prophets*.

7. At an appropriate time, openly share your personal testimony—describe the plan of salvation in detail. Assert that Jesus claimed to be the Son of God repeatedly. Either He is divine or else He is a liar or a lunatic. Since the *Koran* declares Him to be a prophet, how could a righteous prophet lie by attempting to deceive the world regarding His identity.

   Due to entrenched traditions, strong family ties, and extremely strong societal pressures winning Muslims to Christianity is extremely difficult. Be patient. Share truth gradually. Focus on a positive relationship with your Muslim colleagues then, at the appropriate time, share Jesus.

Jehovah's Witnesses

Jehovah's Witnesses grew out of the Millerite movement of the 1840's. The organizer of
the movement, Charles Taze Russell (1852-
1916) had been influenced as a young man
by William Miller. Witnesses emphasize absolute obedience to the one God, Jehovah,
aggressive door to door and street corner
evangelism, and the dramatic establishment of God's Kingdom through the final
Battle of Armageddon. They believe that
Christ will reign on earth during the millennium (all during which resurrection and
judgment will take place). Witnesses are
distinct from mainline evangelical Christians since they reject the Trinity as a pagan
doctrine. They believe that Jesus was not
God, but the Son of God, the first of all God's
creation. They see the Holy Spirit as the
power of God or an impersonal force.

Jehovah's Witnesses carry on an aggressive
publishing work. Their magazines *Watch-
tower* and *Awake* have a combined circulation of well over 10 million representing the
largest publication of a religious journal in
America. After the death of Charles Taze
Russell, a new leader, Joseph F. Rutherford
developed new missionary techniques of
door-to-door ministry combined with dis-
tributing free *Watch Tower* and *Awake* magazines. Each witness is urged to attend three
or four meetings at Jehovah's Witnesses
Kingdom Halls per week and put in a minimum of 10 hours per month in door-to-door
ministry. Accepting the Biblical doctrine of
the priesthood of all believers, Witnesses
believe that baptism is ordination into
ministry. Each member accepts the fact
that he/she is a minister of Jehovah. Mid-
week meetings in Kingdom Halls are often
training sessions for ministry. Jehovah's

Witnesses also reject birthdays, Christmas and Easter as pagan holidays. They refuse to give blood, salute the flag or say the Pledge of Allegiance based on what they perceive to be exclusive obedience to God. Although Jehovah's Witnesses claim to have no paid ministry, they do have "overseers" or traveling ministers who visit the approximately 22 congregations making it a circuit or district. These "ministers" are paid a salary.

Some doctrinal beliefs held in common with Jehovah Witnesses

1. The Priesthood of all believers—all are called to witness.

2. The state of the dead—human beings do not have an immortal soul. Death is a sleep.

3. The annihilation of the wicked—God will not burn sinners in hell for millions of years. They are ultimately consumed.

4. Baptism is by immersion.

5. Signs of the times—world conditions indicate the end of all things is at hand.

Some major doctrinal misunderstandings of Jehovah's Witnesses and Bible texts to meet them

1. **There is only one God Jehovah:** Jesus is a lesser god proceeding forth from the Father. To meet this error please note the following:

   a. Either Jesus is fully God or not God at all. (Isa 43:10)

   b. Who Is Jehovah?

Jehovah Is	**Jesus is**
Glory *(Isa. 42:8)*	Glory *(Matt. 16:27)*
Creator *(Isa. 40:28)*	Creator *(Eph. 3:9)*
Redeemer *(Isa. 33:22)*	Redeemer *(Acts 4:12)*

Judge *(Isa. 33:22)*	Judge *(Jn. 5:22)*
King *(Isa. 33:22)*	King *(Rev. 19:11-16)*
Rock *(Deut. 32:3,4)*	Rock *(1 Cor. 10:4)*
Beginning and	Beginning and
Ending *(Isa. 41:4)*	Ending *(Rev. 1:8-11)*

c. These texts indicate that the New Testament uses the same descriptions of Jesus as the Old Testament does for Jehovah. Jehovah is the family name for God, sometimes applying to the Father but encompassing also the work of His son. *Deut. 6:4* declares the Lord (Jehovah) our God (*Elohim,* plural) is **one** (*Echad*— compound unity indicating the fusion of two equals like day and night for **one** day, or man and woman **one** flesh) is **one** (compound unity) Jehovah.

d. Who Is Jesus?

   (1.) Testimony of Prophet Isaiah *(Isa. 9:6)*.

   (2.) Testimony of angels *(Matt. 1:21)*.

   (3.) Testimony of Thomas *(Jn. 20:26-28)*.

   (4.) Testimony of Jews *(Lk. 5:21; Jn. 10:33)*.

   (5.) Testimony of Jesus "I AM" *(Jn. 8:58,59)*. "I AM" is the self-existent one only applied to Jehovah *(Ex. 3:14)*.

   (6.) Testimony of the Father *(Heb. 1:7-9)*. The Father calls the Son God.

e. Jesus as first born (compare *Col. 1:15* with *Heb. 1:6*).

   (1.) Jesus is called the first born from the dead. Was Jesus the first person to be resurrected from the dead? No *(Lk. 7:11-15; 8:41,42,49-55; Jn. 11:38-44)*.

   (2.) Obviously first-born from the dead does not mean the one raised first but the one raised with the special privilege of power over death.

(3.) David was the youngest son of Jesse but said to be the first born *(Ps. 89:20,27).*

(4.) The Greek word *"Prototokos"* means first born in the sense of privilege, not chronological order. It refers to first born in the sense that Jesus has the rights, privileges, and authority of the first born. In ancient Israel first born had the privilege of representing the Father. Jesus came to reveal God's glory *(Jn. 14:9).*

f. Jesus as the Only Begotten.

Jn. 3:16—the Greek word is *Monogenes* which means "One of a Kind" or "Unique One." Jesus is unique in all of creation. He is one of a kind—the divine son of God, the eternal one dwelling in human flesh revealing the Father in our midst.

g. Jesus as beginning of the creation of God.

(1.) Beginning of creation of God—the Greek word is *Arche.* Jesus is the beginner or origin of God's creation *(Rev. 3:14).*

(2.) All things were made by Him *(Jn. 1:3).*

(3.) By Him all things were created *(Col. 1:16,17; Heb. 11:3).*

2. The law was done away in Christ:

(See *Matt. 5:17,18; Jn. 14:15; Rom. 6:13,14; 3:28-31; Ps. 40:8; Heb. 8:10; 1 Jn. 2:3-6; Jas. 2:10-17.)*

3. Christ's personal presence was revealed in a spiritual Second Coming in

1914. Witnesses believe the word *Parousia* describes the invisible presence of Jesus.

Note: Under Judge Rutherford's leadership, Witnesses taught that the Biblical prophets mentioned in *Heb. 11* such as Abraham, Isaac, and Jacob would be resurrected to live in the Biblical House of Princes shortly after 1914. In fact Rutherford claimed that this would occur in 1925 and published the idea in his book, *Millions Now Living Will Never Die*. Throughout their history Jehovah's Witnesses have continued to set dates for the final Battle of Armageddon, the glorious return of Christ (which they separate from His *parousia* or invisible presence to establish His kingdom). Up until 1975 they taught that the literal Battle of Armageddon would occur in that year. (See *Awake Magazine,* Oct. 8, 1968, for a chart depicting 1975 as the year of the end).

Meaning of *Parousia*: a technical Greek term describing the personal arrival or presence of a person. Never in the Bible does it describe invisible presence *(Matt. 24:3)*.

a. *1 Cor. 16:17*—The *Parousia* or coming of Stephanos was a real or literal event.

b. *2 Pet. 1:16*—Jesus first *Parousia* was a literal or personal event.

c. *Lk. 24:36-43,51*—Jesus ascended with a resurrected glorious body. He will descend the same way.

4. **How Jesus will return**

(See *Matt. 24:27; 1 Thess. 4:16,17; Ps. 50:3; Rev. 1:7; Matt. 24:30; 16:27,28; 13:24-30.*)

When Christ comes the world as we know it will be destroyed *(2 Pet. 3:10; 2 Thess. 1:7-9)*.

The resurrection will occur when Jesus returns *(1 Cor. 15:51-54)*.

5. **The days of creation were 7,000 years long.**

   a. The Hebrew word for day is *Yom*. Every time a numeral precedes the word "day" such as first day, second day, third day, etc. by rules of Hebrew grammar it must be a twenty-four hour period.

   b. *Ps. 33:6,9* and *Heb. 11:3* indicates that creation was an instantaneous event, not a process over thousands of years.

   c. If each day were 7,000 years, since the days of creation were divided into equal parts of light and darkness they would consist of 3,500 years of darkness and 3,500 years of light. Consequently all plant and animal life would have died without light during the lengthy periods of darkness before creation week was over.

   d. The commandments clearly indicate that Jehovah Himself declared creation consists of seven 24-hour periods (See *Ex. 20:11*).

Suggestions for working with Jehovah's Witnesses

1. Assert that everything must come directly from the Bible *(Jn. 17:17)*.

2. Choose one topic and one topic only to discuss.

3. Give them an opportunity to present their version for 30 minutes.

4. Ask questions then present your view for 30 minutes. This enables a complete train of thought to be presented on a single subject rather than jumping from topic to topic.

5. Do not begin with the Trinity. Choose a subject such as Who Is Jesus? the Second Coming of Christ, or Creation.

6. Strongly emphasize the peace that comes from knowing Jesus. Since Jehovah's Witnesses are in bondage to legalism, the Gospel is the real answer.

God's heart longs over the Jewish nation.
Jerusalem is the city He wept over *(Lk.
19:41)*. The Old Testament Scriptures are
filled with promises of both blessings and
curses for the Jewish nation. *(Deut. 28)*
Throughout the Bible, obedience has resulted in abundance while disobedience has
resulted in her people being scattered, tor-
tured, and martyred. Two thousand years
ago, Jesus came to His own people but they
did not receive Him *(Jn. 1:11)*. Rejecting the
Messiah, the Jewish leaders sealed the
nation's destiny. Their cup of iniquity was
full. God established the Christian church as
His new Israel, a kingdom of priests to share
the gospel of love and forgiveness with the
world *(Dan. 9:23-27; Matt. 23:37,38)*. Although Israel as a nation rejected His love
and corporately is no longer His formal chosen people, the Bible predicts scores of Jews
will one day accept God's last day message
(Rom. 11:23,24). In God's eyes, His church is
spiritual Israel. Those who accept Christ
and His truth become Jews according to the
promise given to Abraham *(Gal. 3:27-29)*.
Ellen White also predicts that many Jews
will accept Christ and assist in preparing the
world for His soon return.

"There will be many converted from among
the Jews, and these converts will aid in
preparing the way of the Lord, and making
straight in the desert a highway for our
God." *(Evangelism,* p. 574).

When the loud cry of the angel of *Revelation
18* illuminates the world through the
preaching and living of the gospel by Christ's
church, thousands of Jews will be converted
in a day as at Pentecost. Now is the time to
kindly reach out to our Jewish neighbors in
the spirit of God's love.

Key facts in ancient Jewish history

1. Abraham—called by God to become the spiritual Father of God's people (2000 B.C.).

   (See *Gen. 12:1-9.*)

2. Egyptian bondage (approximately 1875 B.C. to 1445 B.C.—430 years).

   (See *Ex. 12:40; Gal. 3:17.*)

3. Moses—leads Israel from Egyptian bondage (15th century B.C.).

4. David—Israel's most glorious period. During the kingdom period, David prepared for the building of the temple and Solomon accomplished it (1000 B.C.).

5. Nebuchadnezzar—attacked Jerusalem. Scores of intelligent young Hebrews, including Daniel, were led into captivity (605 B.C.).

6. Cyrus—defeated Babylon allowing Israelites to go free (538 B.C.).

7. Babylonian captivity (605 B.C. to 535 B.C.).

   (See *Dan. 9:1,2; 2 Chron. 36:21.*)

8. Destruction of Jerusalem—by Titus (70 A.D.).

Judaism Today

Judaism today may be divided into four main groups:

a. *Secular Jews*—Often atheistic viewpoint, Jewish by traditional upbringing of birth and descent.

b. *Liberal/Reform Jews*—Broad view of scriptures observance of Sabbath, holidays as traditions, usually do not observe Jewish dietary laws.

c. *Conservative Jews*—Emphasize the preservation of Judaism by passing on centuries old traditions with an updated version of Jewish life for contemporary society.

d. *Orthodox Jews*—Ultra-strict, most conservative in diet, dress, Sabbath-keeping and Jewish feasts. Some are strongly Zionistic.

Some Doctrinal truths held in common with Jews

1. Healthful living
2. An understanding of death
3. An appreciation of the Old Testament scriptures
4. The Seventh-day Sabbath
5. The belief that the Messiah will come.

Possible approaches for Jews

1. Develop a caring friendship. Express appreciation for Jewish culture and history. Share your conviction that the ancient Hebrew prophets were inspired by God.

2. Share with your Jewish friend that you believe God has made of "one blood" all nations. Both Christians and Jews are descendants from Abraham.

3. Express the thought openly that Seventh-day Adventists see themselves as spiritual Jews. We accept the dietary laws of the Old Testament as well as the Biblical Sabbath.

4. Discuss only those points we hold in common during your early visits. Our Jewish friends often appreciate good reading material. Books especially helpful include *Flee the Captor* by John Weidner, *Israel's Pre-existent* Messiah and *Daniel's Prophetic Jig-saw Puzzle* by Robert Odom, *The Quest of a Jew* by Samuel Jacobson, *The Almost Forgotten Day* by Mark A. Finley, *Patriarchs and*

Prophets and *Prophets and Kings* by Ellen G. White.

5. Invite your Jewish friends to a *Breathe-Free Plan to Stop Smoking*, nutrition series or vegetarian cooking school. Health programs are excellent events to break down prejudice.

6. When you actually enter into religious discussion with your Jewish friends, ask questions such as the following:

   a. In your opinion, what brought about the prosperity of the nation of Israel during Bible times? Why did God allow the Egyptian bondage, the Babylonian captivity, and the destruction of Jerusalem? *(See Deut. 28; Jer. 17.)*

   b. Who was Isaiah the prophet talking about in *Isa. 53*? Read *Isa. 53* aloud with your friend.

   c. Review the Old Testament prophecies relating to the Messiah in *Dan. 9:23-27; Mic. 5:2; Isa. 9:6; 7:14; Ps. 22;* and *Gen. 49:10.*

   d. Share your testimony describing the peace, forgiveness, freedom from guilt and assurance of salvation that Jesus gives you personally.

   e. Invite your Jewish friend to systematically study the ancient prophecies of Daniel with you.

   Many Christians have a difficult time relating to the Jews. Following the principles outlined above, you will find contacts with your Jewish friends extremely rewarding.

Lutherans

Lutheranism grew out of Catholicism in the 16th century. The powerful teachings of Martin Luther coupled with the power of the German princes who supported him, created a major break from the authority of Rome. Luther believed in the supremacy of the Word above tradition. He emphasized salvation by grace alone in Christ, the Priesthood of all believers, and man's innate sinfulness and lostness without God's free gift. Luther saw the whole point of Christ's coming as to bring salvation. Human beings could not earn it by themselves. Luther's translation of the New Testament, published in 1522, and the Old Testament, in 1534, quickly became best sellers as they were widely circulated through Germany. Luther found no basis in the Bible for a celibate priesthood, so broke with tradition and married a former nun. His heart burned with the desire to proclaim God's Word as final authority on matters of faith and doctrines. Today, there are over 10 separate Lutheran bodies with close to 10 million members in America. Through the years Lutheranism has become significantly more liberal in its approach to the scriptures. There are a variety of beliefs within Lutheranism today. Some deny the virgin birth, question a literal seven-day creation week, reject a universal flood, and seriously wonder about Jesus' Second Coming. Most Lutherans are not the careful Bible students they were in former years.

Some doctrinal beliefs held in common with Lutherans

1. The authority of God's Word.

2. Salvation by grace alone.

3. The literal Second Coming of Christ.

4. The Godhead.

5. Obedience to God.

Some major doctrinal misunderstandings of Lutherans and Bible texts to meet them

1. **Baptism by sprinkling:**

   (See *Matt. 28:19,20; Mk. 16:16; Matt. 3:13-17; Acts 8:26-38; Jn. 3:22; Rom. 6:1-8; Col. 2:12.*)

2. **Immortality of the soul:** The belief that each individual has an immortal, indestructible soul distinct from the body but which leaves the body at death destined for heaven or hell.

   (See *1 Tim. 6:15,16; Gen. 2:7; Eccl. 12:7; Job 27:3; Ps. 146:4; 6:5; 115:17; Jn. 11:11-14.)* Remember the Bible uses the word "soul" 1,600 times and never *once* says "immortal soul." The Bible calls death a sleep 53 times.

3. **Sunday sacredness:** The belief that since Jesus rose from the dead on the first day, all Christians should worship on that day.

   (See *Gen. 2:1-3; Ex. 20:8-11; Ezek. 20:12,20; Lk. 4:16; Matt. 24:20; Acts 13:42-44; Rev. 1:10; Matt. 12:8; Lk. 6:5; Isa. 66:22,23.)*

4. **Church/state relations:** Luther believed in strong cooperation between church and state. He saw the church used of God to influence Christian legislation.

5. **Communion:** Lutherans place great emphasis on what they call con-substantiation or Christ's real presence in the communion bread. The Bible teaches that communion is a symbol of Christ's death received by faith *(1 Cor. 11:23-28)*. The "I AM" statements of Jesus do not denote literal presence. Comparison: "I am the light," "I am the good

shepherd," "I am the Vine," "I am the Rock," suggests a symbolic description of one aspect of Christ's work.

Approaches to the Lutheran mind

1. Develop a strong bond of friendship. Emphasize the authority of scripture. Affirm that salvation is only through Christ. Make it plain that you believe salvation is only by grace through faith in Christ.

2. Present the prophecies to clearly establish God's Word *(Dan. 2; Matt. 24*, divinity of Christ).

3. As soon as possible enter into systematic, regular Bible studies.

4. Lutherans often have a clear view of the plan of salvation but never have been exposed to a detailed Biblical study of the prophecies.

5. Emphasize the fact that obedience is always response to God's love. His love constrains us *(2 Cor. 5:14)*. It causes us to do things —the Saviour has declared "If you love me keep my commandments *(Jn. 14:15)*. Love always leads to obedience *(Rom. 13:10)*. It always responds positively to God's commands *(Rev. 14:12)*.

6. The essential issue for each Lutheran is whether they will follow additional light going beyond Luther or lose what they once had *(Jn. 12:35)*. Light is progressive *(Prov. 4:18)*. It keeps moving on.

7. A study on "Why so many Denominations" (the need for continually following more light is always helpful.)

Methodists

The regular church life of Lutherans and
Calvinists had taken on a certain rigid for-
mality in the mid-17th and 18th century.
Methodism grew out of German pietistic
movements who emphasized

1. A Bible-centered faith.

2. The genuine Christian life

3. Free expression of faith in hymns, testimonies and evangelical zeal.

Methodism's founder, John Wesley (1703-
1791) attended Oxford University to study
for the ministry. While at Oxford, he founded
a religious society called "The Holy Club" (by
other students). Since their habits were extremely disciplined and strict, they earned
the title of the Methodists. After his miraculous conversion at the Aldersgate Chapel
on May 24, 1738, due to a lay preacher reading Luther's epistle to the Romans, he established Methodist societies throughout
England. These societies placed emphasis
on holiness, growth in grace, and living the
Christian life. In an age of religious formalism, Wesley's teachings were like a breath of
Christian fresh air. Today there are between
10 and 11 million Methodists in the United
States. The piety of the past is generally
gone. A significant number of Methodists
today doubt the fundamentals of Christianity such as the virgin birth, the divinity of
Christ, creation, the flood, the miracles of
Christ, and the Second Coming.

Some doctrinal truths held in common with Methodists

1. The Godhead (Trinity).

2. Salvation by grace.

3. Emphasis on holiness, sanctification and growth in grace.

4. Reject eternally burning hell.

5. Celebrate the Lord's supper.

Some major doctrinal misunderstandings of Methodists and Bible texts to meet them

1. **Reject literal Second Coming:**

   (See *1 Thess. 4:16,17; Rev. 1:7; Matt. 16:17; Matt. 24:27*)

2. **Immortality of the soul:** The belief that each individual has an immortal, indestructible soul distinct from the body but which leaves the body at death destined for heaven or hell.

   (See *1 Tim. 6:15,16; Gen. 2:7; Eccl. 12:7; Job 27:3; Ps. 146:4; 6:5; 115:17; John 11:11-14.*) Remember the Bible uses the word "soul" 1,600 times and never *once* says "immortal soul." The Bible calls death a sleep 53 times.

3. **Sunday sacredness:** The belief that since Jesus rose from the dead on the first day, all Christians should worship on that day.

   (See *Gen. 2:1-3; Ex. 20:8-11; Ezek. 20:12,20; Lk. 4:16; Matt. 24:20; Acts 13:42-44; Rev. 1:10; Matt. 12:8; Lk. 6:5; Isa. 66:22,23.*)

4. **Infant baptism/adult baptism:** although occasionally adult believers are baptized by immersion the church has officially retained sprinkling in the creed.

   (See *Matt. 28:19,20; Mk. 16:16; Jn. 3:5; Acts 2:38-41; Acts 8:26-38; Col. 2:12; Rom. 6:1-8.*)

5. **Many reject the authority of the Bible.** Many Methodists have serious doubts about the inspiration of the Old and New Testa-

ments. They believe the Bible contains the *Word of God* but question whether it *is* in *fact* the Word of God. Often they believe it is historically and culturally conditioned.

(See *Jn. 17:17; 2 Tim. 3:16,17; 2 Pet. 1:20,21; Matt. 4:4.*)

Approaches for the Methodist Mind

1. Emphasize their roots and similarity with Adventists. Express appreciation for Wesley's concept that grace is free to all. God doesn't merely choose a few who will be saved. Discuss the fact that Wesley rightly understood the need for Christian growth, sanctification, and holiness in the life.

2. Mention that Methodism, like many churches, has tended to drift from its former heritage.

3. Studies on the authority and inspiration of the Bible, *Dan. 2,* and *Matt. 24* establish the credibility of the Bible.

4. As soon as possible enter into weekly systematic Bible study discussions.

Note: The Methodist organizational structure of conferences is similar to the Adventist organizational structure. Scores of early Adventists had Methodist backgrounds, thus we see reflected within Adventism a strong influence from Methodism in both our understanding of doctrine and organizational structure. This is still one more evidence that God's light is progressive.

Mormons
(Church of Jesus Christ of Latter-Day Saints)

The founder of the church, Joseph Smith claimed that in the spring of 1820 he had a vision in which he saw God and Jesus Christ. He was told not to join any church but to establish the church of Christ in its fullness. In September of 1823, the angel Moroni purportedly appeared to Smith in a vision to tell him that a book containing the history of the ancient inhabitants of America was buried in a hill called Cumorah, about four miles from Palmyra, New York. The next day Smith supposedly found the book. Although not allowed to look at it until 1827, he eventually translated its golden plates. Combined with visions and revelation, its teachings formed the basis for the *Book of Mormon*. Smith wrote two other books, *Doctrine and Covenants* and *The Pearl of Great Price*. Mormons are industrious, hard working, morally upright, temperate people, yet most of their doctrines find little harmony with the Bible.

Mormons believe:

1. The Bible is the Word of God only as far as it is correctly translated. They believe the Book of Mormon is superior to the Bible because the words are "pure" words.

2. Man pre-existed with God as an immortal soul before being created. One of the reasons for creation was to create bodies for these souls.

3. God was pleased when Adam and Eve sinned because the earth would now be populated.

4. There are immortal souls now living in the Spirit world with Jesus preaching the gospel to them.

5. They must hold baptismal services for the dead in Mormon Temples.

6. Jesus was married to Mary, Martha, and the other Mary at the wedding feast of Cana (*Journal of Discourses*, vol. 4, p. 259, by Brigham Young). They accept polygamy or multiple marriages where the law of the land permits it.

7. Marriage must be sealed for time and eternity in a Mormon Temple.

8. There are three degrees of heaven—the *celestial* (for faithful Mormons), the *terrestrial* (for Mormons not so faithful), and the *telestral* (for others who will be servants). In essence all humanity will receive eternal life yet some will become servants of others.

Some doctrinal beliefs held in common with Mormons

1. Mormons are faithful tithe payers.

2. Mormons are concerned about their health, refraining from alcohol and tobacco.

3. Mormons accept the concept of the Gift of Prophecy in the church today.

4. Mormons believe in baptism by immersion.

5. Mormons accept the idea that the religious bodies today are "fallen Babylon" and Christianity needs a return to New Testament teachings.

Some major doctrinal misunderstandings of Mormons and Bible texts to meet them

1. **The Bible is mistranslated**

   (See *2 Tim. 3:15,16; Jn. 17:17; 5:39; Ps. 12:6; 2 Pet. 1:21; Matt. 4:4.*)

2. **Baptism for the dead:** A belief based on a misunderstanding of *1 Cor. 15:29.* In the

New Testament baptism is always a personal decision indicating belief in Christ, repentance from sin, and acceptance of Jesus teachings.

(See *Acts 2:38-41; Mk. 16:16; Matt. 28:19,20.*)

In the New Testament salvation is based on a personal choice. No one can provide that opportunity for another.

(See *Rev. 22:17; Ps. 49:7.*)

In *1 Cor. 15:29* the apostle Paul is arguing in favor of the resurrection. He thus raises a question. If the dead are not raised at all, why then are you baptized for (Greek translation in behalf of, or because of)? When Christ returns the dead in Christ will be resurrected and the righteous living caught up with them to meet Jesus in the air (*1 Thess. 4:16,17*). To be baptized in behalf of or because of the dead means to be baptized as a result of their godly influence and Christian lives and thus prepare to meet them in eternity.

(See *Heb. 11: 39,40.*)

3. **Sunday worship:** Mormons believe that the first day of the week, Sunday, is called "The Sabbath" eight times in the original Greek Bible. This is based on a total misunderstanding of the word for week which comes from the same root word in the original as the word for Sabbath, but is a different word.

   (See *Gen. 2:1-3; Ex. 20:8-11; Ezek. 20:20; Lk. 4:16; Matt. 24:20; Acts 13:42-44; Lk. 6:5; Matt. 12:8; Isa. 66:22,23.*)

4. **Immortality of the soul:** The belief that each individual has an immortal, indestructible soul distinct from the body but which leaves the body at death destined for heaven or hell.

(See *1 Tim. 6:15,16; Gen. 2:7; Eccl. 12:7; Job 27:3; Ps. 146:4; 6:5; 115:17; Jn. 11:11-14.*) Remember the Bible uses the word "soul" 1,600 times and never *once* says "immortal soul." The Bible calls death a sleep 53 times.

Possible approaches to the Mormon mind

1. Develop a close bond of friendship.

2. Invite them over for a meal.

3. Mormons have extremely close family ties, therefore respect the family unit by inviting the entire family to study the Bible with you.

4. Present a study on the Inspiration of the Bible.

5. Share your personal testimony with Jesus Christ.

6. After 3-5 weeks of study present the topic "Is the Gospel of Mormonism the Gospel of the Bible?"

7. Lovingly appeal to your Mormon friends to follow the true Christ.

To assist you in your work with Mormons I have included a Bible study entitled "Is the Gospel of Mormonism the Gospel of the Bible?" You will find the teachings of the Mormon Church preceeded by Bible texts which clearly expose the error of these teachings.

Is the Gospel of Mormonism the Gospel of the Bible?

Was Jesus conceived by the Holy Ghost?

Biblical response: *Matt. 1:18-21; Lk. 1:35.*

Mormon response:

Brigham Young, the second president of the Mormon Church, once stated:

"Now remember from this time forth and for ever, that *Jesus Christ **was not begotten by the Holy Ghost**" (Journal of Discourses*, vol. 1, p. 51).

Joseph Fielding Smith, President of the Twelve Apostles, has denied that the *Book of Mormon* and the Bible teach that Christ was begotten by the Holy Ghost. He stated as follows:

"They tell us the *Book of Mormon* states that Jesus was begotten of the Holy Ghost. *I challenge that statement*. The book of Mormon *teaches **no such thing!*** neither does the Bible." (*Doctrines of Salvation*, vol. 1. p. 19).

Was Jesus born of a virgin?

Biblical response: *Isa. 9:6; Isa. 7:14.*

Mormon response:

In a discourse delivered, April, 9, 1852, Brigham Young declared:

"When the Virgin Mary conceived the child Jesus, the Father had begotten him in his own likeness. *He was not begotten by the Holy Ghost. And who is the Father? **He is the first of the human family;**....*I could tell you much more about this; but were I to tell you the whole truth, **blasphemy would be nothing to it,** in the estimation of the superstitious and over-righteous of mankind. However, I have told you **the truth** as far as*

> *I have gone. ... Jesus our elder brother, was begotten in the flesh by the same character that was in the Garden of Eden,* and who is our Father in heaven. Now, let all who may hear these doctrines, pause before they make light of them, or treat them with indifference, for *they will prove their salvation or damnation."* (*Journal of Discourses*, vol. 1, pp. 50-51)

This same type of reasoning led the Apostle Orson Pratt to say:

"The fleshly body of Jesus required a mother as well as a father. Therefore, the father and mother of Jesus, according to the flesh must have been *associated together in the capacity of husband and wife; hence the virgin Mary must have been, for the time being, the lawful wife of God the Father*: we use the term lawful wife, because it would be blasphemous in the highest degree to say that he overshadowed her or begat a Saviour unlawfully:....He had a lawful right to overshadow the Virgin Mary in the capacity of a husband, and begat a son, although she was espoused to another: for the law *which he gave to govern men and women was not intended to govern himself*, or to prescribe rules for his own conduct. It was also lawful in him after having thus dealt with Mary, to give her to Joseph her espoused husband. Whether God the Father gave Mary to Joseph for time only or for time and eternity, we are not informed. *Inasmuch as God was the first husband to her*, it may be that he only gave her to be the wife of Joseph while in the mortal state, *and that he intended after the resurrection to take her as his wife in eternity. (The Seer*, p. 158).

Brigham Young explained the birth of Christ as follows:

"The birth of the Saviour was as natural as are the births of our children: *it was the result of natural action.* He partook of flesh and blood—was begotten of his Father, as we are of our fathers" (*Journal of Discourses*, vol. 8, p. 115).

Heber C. Kimball, who was a member of the First Presidency of the Mormon Church, made this statement:

In relation to the way in which I look upon the works of God and his creatures, I will say that *I was naturally begotten; so was my father, and also my Saviour Jesus Christ.* According to the Scriptures, he is the first begotten of his father in the flesh, and there was *nothing unnatural about it*" (*Journal of Discourses*, vol. 8, p. 211).

Where is the source of Salvation?

Biblical response: *Jn. 14:6; Acts 4:12.*

Mormon response:

"Unconditional or general salvation, that which comes by grace alone without obedience to gospel law, consists in the mere fact of being resurrected...This kind of salvation eventually will come to all mankind...This is not the salvation of righteousness, the salvation which the saints seek. Those who gain only this general or unconditional salvation will be judged according to their works...They will ...be dammed...in eternity (they) will be ministering servants to more worthy persons" (*Mormon Doctrine*, p. 669).

Immortality not eternal life: "Conditional or individual salvation, that which comes by grace coupled with gospel obedience consists in receiving an inheritance in the celestial kingdom, however, those who *do not go on to exaltation* will have *immortality only,* and *not eternal life*...They *will live separately* and *singly in an unmarried state*...

"Full salvation is attained by virtue of knowledge, truth, righteousness, and all true principles...Without the atonement, the gospel, the priesthood, and the sealing power, there would be no salvation. Without continuous revelation...there would be no salvation. If it had not been for Joseph Smith and the restoration, there would be no salvation.

"There is no salvation outside The Church of Jesus Christ of Latter-day Saints." (*Mormon Doctrine*, pp. 669-670)

Are there sins too great for the blood of Christ to atone?

Biblical response: *1 Pet. 2:20-24.*

Mormon response:

In the book, *Doctrines of Salvation*, Joseph Fielding Smith states:

"Joseph Smith taught that there were certain sins so grievous that man may commit, that *they will place the transgressors **beyond the power of the atonement of Christ***. If these offenses are committed, then the blood of Christ *will not **cleanse*** them from their sins *even though they repent. Therefore their only hope is to have their blood shed to atone,* as far as possible, in their behalf.....

"And men for certain crimes have *had to atone* as far as they could for their sins wherein *they have placed themselves **beyond the redeeming power of the blood of Christ***" (*Doctrines of Salvation*, vol. 1, pp. 135-136).

How can such sins be forgiven?

Biblical response: *Jn. 3:16; Gal. 2:20; 1 Jn. 1:7-9; Matt. 12:32.*

Mormon response:

Brigham Young, the second President of the
Mormon Church, said:

"There are **sins** that men commit for which
they cannot receive forgiveness in this world,
or in that which is to come, and if they had
their eyes open to see their true condition,
they would be perfectly willing to **have** *their
blood spilt* upon the ground, that the smoke
thereof might ascend to heaven as an *offering for their sins*; and the smoking incense
would *atone* for their sins, whereas, if such
is not the case, they will stick to them and
remain upon them in the spirit world.

"I know, when you *hear my brethren* telling
*about **cutting people off from the earth**,
that you consider it is strong doctrine, but it
is to **save** them, not to destroy them ...

"And furthermore, I know that there are
transgressors, who, if they knew themselves, and the *only condition* upon which
they can obtain forgiveness, *would beg of
their brethren to shed their blood* that the
smoke thereof might ascend to God as an
offering to appease the wrath that is kindled
against them, and that the law might have
its course. I will say further; *I have had men
come to me, and offer their lives to atone for
their sins.*

"It is true that the blood of the Son of God
was shed for sins through the fall and those
committed by men, *yet men can commit sins
which it can never remit.* As it was in ancient
days, so it is in our day; and though the
principles are taught publicly from this
stand, still the people do not understand the;
yet the law is precisely the same. There are
sins that can be **atoned** for by an offering
upon an altar, as in ancient days; and there
are sins that the blood of a lamb, of a calf, or
of turtle doves, cannot remit, but *they must
be atoned for by the blood of the man*. That is

the reason why men talk to you as they do from this stand; they understand *the doctrine* and throw out a few words about it. You have been *taught that doctrine,* but you do not understand it." (Sermon by Brigham Young, *Journal of Discourses,* vol. 4, pp. 53-54; *Desert News,* 1856, p. 235).

Can individuals be saved in their sins— without repentance and confession?

Biblical response: *Acts 16:30,31; Acts 3:19,20.*

Mormon response:

Brigham Young, the second President of the Mormon Church, stated:

*"Let me suppose a case. Suppose you found your brother in bed with your wife, and **put a javelin through both of them, you would be justified, and they would atone for their sins, and be received into the kingdom of god.** I would at once do so* in such a case; and under such circumstances, *I have no wife whom I love so well that I would not put a javelin through her heart, and I would **do it with clean hands**...*

"There is not a man or woman, who violates the covenants made with their God, that will not be required to pay the debt. The blood of Christ will never wipe that out, *your own blood must atone for it...*" (*Journal of Discourses,* vol, 3, p. 247)

What about the present? Joseph Fielding Smith, official historian of the Mormon Church in recent years, has been the "Spokesman" for many years through his writings. He says:

"But men may commit certain grievous sins...that will place *him beyond the reach of the atoning blood of Christ...*Therefore their only hope is to have *their own blood shed to atone...*" (*Doctrines of Salvation,* vol. 1, pp. 134-135, Joseph Fielding Smith,).

Does this mean the individuals blood must be shed?

Joseph Fielding Smith, the Mormon historian, makes this statement concerning the doctrine of "Blood Atonement":

"Just a word or two now, *on the subject of* **blood atonement**. What is that doctrine? Unadulterated, if you please, laying aside the pernicious insinuations and lying charges that have so often been made, it is simply this: Through the atonement of Christ all mankind may be saved, by obedience to the laws and ordinances of the gospel.....

"But man may commit certain grievous sins —according to his light and knowledge — that *will place him **beyond** the reach of the atoning blood of Christ. If then he would be saved he must make sacrifice of his own life to atone*—so far as in his power lies—for that sin, for the blood of Christ *alone* under certain circumstances will *not avail*." (*Ibid. pp. 133-134*).

Bruce McConkie, of the First Council of Seventy, stated as follows in his book, *Mormon Doctrine*: "...under certain circumstances there are *some serious sins* for which the *cleansing of Christ does not operate*, and the **law of god is that men must have their own blood shed to atone for their sins**..." (*p. 87*).

B. H. Roberts, who was a Mormon Church historian, described the doctrine of blood atonement as follows: "...what is needful for the **salvation** *of the soul* where one's *sins place him **beyond** the reach of vicarious means of salvation—then it is the **shedding of the sinner's own blood** that must here be referred to" (*A Comprehensive History of the Church*, by B. H. Roberts, vol. 4, p. 129).

Is this love?

Biblical response: *1 Jn. 4:8-10,19-21.*

Mormon response:

> ***This is loving your brother***: "(S)uppose that he is overtaken in a gross fault...that he knows will deprive him of what exaltation...that he cannot attain to it *without the shedding of his blood,* and also knows that by having his blood shed, he will atone for that sin, and be saved and exalted with the Gods, is there a man or woman in this house but what would say 'shed my blood that I may be saved and exalted with the Gods?'"

> "*Will you love* that man or woman well enough to *shed their blood*? I could refer you to *plenty of instances* where men have been *righteously slain,* in order *to atone* for their *sins....*the wickedness and ignorance of the nations forbids this principle's being in full force, but *the time will come,* when the law of God will be in full force.

> "*This is loving our neighbor as ourselves;* if he needs help, help him; and if he wants salvation and it is necessary to *spill his blood....*that he may be saved, ***spill it...That is the way to love mankind*"** (Prophet Brigham Young, discourse delivered February 8, 1857. Printed in *Desert News*, February 18, 1857, also *Journal of Discourses,* vol 4, pp. 219-220).

Nazarenes

The Nazarene church grew out of the Holiness Associations of the Eastern States and California. Organized in Chicago in 1907 they have grown to over 300,000 members in the United States. They have a strong mission emphasis supporting eight colleges and a theological seminary. Conservative, fundamental Christians, the Nazarenes believe in:

1. The Bible as the inspired word of God.

2. The literal Second Coming of Christ.

3. Salvation by faith in Christ alone.

4. The immortality of the soul.

5. Eternal torment.

6. Sunday sacredness.

7. Avoidance of alcohol and tobacco.

8. Separation from the world and a conservative life style.

9. Baptism by immersion.

Nazarenes are fundamental Christians who hold high moral and ethical standards. Believing the Bible is the inspired word of God, they accept it as a moral imperative for life. They have a strong sense that God has raised up their movement to once again elevate the moral standard of Christianity. They see themselves as reformers. Their high Biblical standards are to be commended, yet they have not gone far enough. Unwittingly they still retain the twin errors of the immortality of the soul and Sunday sacredness. In working with this group, be prepared to give a comprehensive Bible study on such subjects as the law, the Sabbath and change, the fall of Babylon, why so many different denominations, as well as the prophetic rise of Adventism. It is our prophetic message and an understanding of *Rev. 10, 12, 14, 17* and *18* which will make a significant impact on Nazarenes.

Some doctrinal beliefs held in common with Nazarenes

1. The Bible is God's Word.

2. The Trinity or Godhead.

3. Salvation only through Christ.

4. The Second Coming of Christ.

5. Sanctification.

6. The necessity for prayer and devotional life.

Some major doctrinal misunderstandings of Nazarenes and Bible texts to meet them

1. **Sunday sacredness:** The belief that since Jesus rose from the dead on the first day, all Christians should worship on that day.

   (See *Gen. 2:1-3; Ex. 20:8-11; Ezek. 20:12-20; Lk. 4:16; Matt. 24:20; Acts 13:42-44; Rev. 1:10; Matt. 12:8; Lk. 6:5; Isa. 66:22,23.*)

2. **Immortality of the soul:** The belief that each individual has an immortal, indestructible soul distinct from the body but which leaves the body at death destined for heaven or hell.

   (See *1 Tim. 6:15,16; Gen. 2:7; Eccl. 12:7; Job 27:3; Ps. 146:4; 6:5; 115:17; Jn. 11:11-14.*) Remember the Bible uses the word "soul" 1,600 times and never *once* says "immortal soul." The Bible calls death a sleep 53 times.

3. **Eternal torment**: The belief that God punishes the lost in hell for eternity.

   (See *Mal. 4:1-3; Ps. 37:10,11,20,38; Jude 7; 2 Pet. 2:6; Rev. 20:9; Heb. 12:29.*)

Possible Approaches to Nazarenes

1. Establish a strong, Christ-centered friendship.

2. Emphasize salvation by Christ alone, the need for Bible support of every teaching and the soon return of Christ.

3. Share a study on the fall of Christianity, apostasy within the church, and God's plan for restoration.

4. Nazarenes will particularly respond to prophetic studies on *Daniel* and *Revelation*.

5. Share a study on *Rev. 14*, going over the three angels' messages step-by-step.

Pentecostals

Pentecostalism is often referred to as "the third force" in Christianity along side traditional Catholicism and historic Protestantism. Pentecostals are rapidly growing throughout the world. Numbering over 100 million in at least 15 major assemblies and many small independent groups, they particularly emphasize the Baptism of the Holy Spirit accompanied by speaking in tongues (glossalalia), divine healing, and the charismatic gifts of the early church. The actual Pentecostal movement began in the United States as an outgrowth of the holiness movement of the late 1800's and early 1900's. The 20th century growth of Pentecostalism is one of the world's remarkable phenomena in modern Christianity. Pentecostals are found all over the world, with large concentrations in South America, Inter-America, and Africa, as well as the United States. Even in secular Europe, Pentecostals are growing. In an age of formalism in many main line religious bodies, the spontaneity, joy, and ferver of Pentecostalism services attract thousands. Shunning elaborate liturgies, they attempt to adhere to the simplicity of the early church. At times their spontaneous services, including testimonies, tongues, and healing, become disorderly.

Some doctrinal beliefs held in common with Pentecostals

1. The Bible as the only rule of faith and practice.

2. Salvation through the blood of Christ.

3. The fact of Jesus' soon return.

4. Baptism by immersion.

5. The Lord's Supper (some practice foot washing).

6. The Virgin Birth.

7. The gifts of the Spirit will be manifest in the church today including the Biblical gift of prophecy.

Some major doctrinal misunderstanding of Pentecostals and Bible texts to meet them

1. **The secret rapture:** The belief that Christ will return secretly prior to the tribulation (plagues) to snatch away or rapture His church leaving the unsaved on earth to suffer through the plagues.

   (See *1 Thess. 4:16,17; 2 Thess. 1:7-9; Matt. 13:30; Lk. 17: 26-37; Rev. 19:12-21; Matt. 24:27; Ps. 50:3; Rev. 1:7.)*

2. **Immortality of the soul:** The belief that each individual has an immortal, indestructible soul distinct from the body but which leaves the body at death destined for heaven or hell.

   (See *1 Tim. 6:15,16; Gen. 2:7; Eccl. 12:7; Job 27:3; Ps. 146:4; 6:5; 115:17; Jn. 11:11-14.)* Remember the Bible uses the word "soul" 1,600 times and never *once* says "immortal soul." The Bible calls death a sleep 53 times.

3. **Once saved always saved:** The belief that once an individual comes to Christ they can never lose their salvation.

   (See *1 Cor. 15:1,2; 2 Pet. 2:20-22; 1 Cor. 9:27* [The word castaway here is the same word used in *Jer. 6:30* for burned or rejected]; *Heb. 4:4-7; Rev. 3:5;* see also *Phil. 4:3*— When we accept Christ, our names are placed in the Book of Life. Since they can be removed, it is possible for those who once accepted to reject.)

Many Pentecostals do not believe once saved always saved, however, you will find individual Pentecostals who believe that once they've spoken in tongues, they are sealed with Christ and cannot be lost. For that reason, we have included this section.

4. **Sunday sacredness:** The belief that since Jesus rose from the dead on the first day, all Christians should worship on that day.

   (See *Gen. 2:1-3; Ex. 20:8-11; Ezek. 20:12,20; Lk. 4:16; Matt. 24:20; Acts 13:42-44; Rev. 1:10; Matt. 12:8; Lk. 6:5; Isa. 66:22,23.)*

6. **Speaking in tongues:** A sign of the infilling of the Holy Spirit manifest in ecstatic utterance (the language of the Holy Spirit) not understood by the speaker but understood only by God. Most Pentecostals believe that without tongues there is no baptism of the Holy Spirit.

   a. Explain to your Pentecostal friend that you believe in the genuine, authentic, Biblical gift of tongues.

   b. Establish that it is God who chooses who receives what gift. The gifts are individually distributed by God as He deems best *(1 Cor. 12:11).*

   c. Point out that everyone does not receive the gift of tongues. Tongues is only one of a long list of gifts and a lesser one at that *(1 Cor. 12: 27-31).*

   d. Love is more important to God than tongues or prophecy. *(1 Cor. 13:1,2)*

   e. The sign of the infilling of the Holy Spirit is a loving heart which desires to witness for Jesus *(Acts 1:6-8).*

   f. Tongues are not specifically given for believers to edify themselves but as a confirmatory sign to convince unbelievers of the gospel *(1 Cor. 14:22).*

g. Tongues are a real language given by God so the language barrier can be broken in the communication of the gospel *(Acts 2:4-11).*

h. In *1 Cor. 14* Paul argues for intelligent speech not unintelligible gibberish *(1 Cor. 14:7-19).*

i. The apostle gives the following controls if tongues are used in the church.

    (1.) Only one person may speak at a time. There should be no spontaneous outbursts with many people speaking at once *(1 Cor. 14:26,27).*

    (2.) No more than two or at the most three people should speak at any given service *(1 Cor. 14:26,27).*

    (3.) There must be an interpreter of the foreign language so the entire congregation will receive the benefit of what is spoken and participate in the worship service together *(1 Cor. 14:28).*

j. The fullness of God's Holy Spirit is poured out upon those who are lovingly obedient to God's truth *(Acts 5:32; Jn. 14:15,16).*

Approaches for the Pentecostal mind

1. In approaching your Pentecostal friends, openly affirm your great love for the Lord.

2. Share with them your personal experience with Jesus as the ground of your assurance for eternal life. Point out the word of God must be the basis of our faith *(Jn. 17:17).*

3. Our emotions are not trustworthy. Some times they are up and other times they are down. Satan can manipulate the emotions. He can even counterfeit genuine miracles or

signs and wonders in an attempt to deceive
(Matt. 24:24; Rev. 16:13,14).

4. Some will declare Christ has worked power-
   fully for them. They will even cast out demons in His name but He will say "I never
   knew you" *(Matt. 7:21-23)*.

5. Faith must be based on God's written word
   if it will stand *(Matt. 7:24)*.

6. Our only safeguard is knowing God's word
   and living by His truth *(Isa. 8:20)*.

7. It is the truth which sets us free from error
   (Jn. 8:32).

8. It is the Holy Spirit which wrote the Bible
   (2 Pet. 1:21).

9. To be filled with the Holy Spirit means to
   accept the words of Jesus as my own *(Jn.
   6:63)*.

10. The greatest miracle is that of a changed
    heart *(Jn. 3:2-7)*.

11. To look for spectacular miracles while re-
    jecting truth is unbiblical *(Lk. 16:27-31)*.

12. Receiving God's truth as revealed in scrip-
    ture is our safeguard against delusion
    (2 Thess. 2:9-12).

Presbyterians

Presbyterians trace their origins to the reformation period and the teachings of John Calvin. Calvin's concept of the sovereignty of God, combined with his understanding of justification by faith, led him to the belief that God has elected some for salvation and others for damnation. In the pre-designed plan of God, some would be saved and others lost. His concept of the sovereignty of God led to a clear distinction between church and state. Calvin believed in religious tolerance for all peoples.

The Presbyterians number approximately 4,500,000 in the United States today. Their system of church government gives autonomy to local congregations allowing them to function independently. The role of ordaining and installing all ministers is the responsibility of a board appointed by a group of congregations called Presbyters. The Synod supervises the Presbyterians. The highest governing body in the Presbyterian Church is the General Assembly made up of pastors and lay delegates from the Presbyters.

Presbyterians are guided in their understanding of truth by the Westminster confession of 1649. In 1967 a more liberalized confession of faith was adopted which emphasizes love, peace, and what God has done in reconciling the world to Himself through Christ. The Presbyterian Church today, as most mainline protestant churches, has significantly softened its previous positions with a de-emphasis on the Bible.

Some doctrinal beliefs held in common with Presbyterians

1. The inspiration of the Bible (although some Presbyterian ministers of a liberal persuasion doubt the integrity of the scriptures).

2. The Trinity or Godhead.

3. Eternal life through Jesus Christ.

4. The Virgin Birth.

5. Heaven.

6. The literal Second Coming of Christ (although some are confused with futurism).

Some major doctrinal misunderstandings of Presbyterians and Bible texts to meet them

1. **Pre-destination:** The general concept that God has pre-designed some people to be saved and others to be lost. This doctrine denies both God's justice, his love, and human freedom of choice *(1 Tim. 2:3-5; 2 Pet. 3:9; Rev. 22:17)*. It is true that God has a pre-designed plan for each individual. This pre-designed plan is to save all mankind. Individuals have the opportunity of choosing whether or not they will accept his plan.

2. **Sunday sacredness:** The belief that since Jesus rose from the dead on the first day, all Christians should worship on that day.

   (See *Gen. 2:1-3; Ex. 20:8-11; Ezek. 20:12,20; Lk. 4:16; Matt. 24:20; Acts 13:42-44; Rev. 1:10; Matt. 12:8; Lk. 6:5; Isa. 66:22,23.)*

3. **Immortality of the soul:** The belief that each individual has an immortal, indestructible soul distinct from the body but which leaves the body at death destined for heaven or hell.

   (See *1 Tim. 6:15,16; Gen. 2:7; Eccl. 12:7; Job 27:3; Ps. 146:4; 6:5; 115:17; Jn. 11:11-*

14.) Remember the Bible uses the word "soul" 1,600 times and never *once* says "immortal soul." The Bible calls death a sleep 53 times.

4. **The inspiration of the Bible:** Since some Presbyterians have a hazy view of the inspiration of scripture. The following passages will be helpful in establishing the authority of the Bible.

(See *2 Tim. 3:16; 2 Pet. 1:21; Isa. 34:16; Ps. 119:105; Jn. 17:17; 2 Sam. 7:28; Prov. 12:6,7.)*

5. **The law was done away in Christ:**

(See *Matt. 5:17,18; Jn. 13:14; Rom. 6:13,14; 3:28-31; Ps. 40:8; Heb. 8:10; 1 Jn. 2:3-6; Jas. 2:10-17.)*

Possible approaches with Presbyterians

1. Demonstrate genuine Christian caring, tact and tenderness.

2. Share articles or booklets on God's love or on a topic of current interest relating to signs of the times.

3. Ask such questions as:

   a. How do you understand the Middle East crisis?

   b. Can you make any sense out of what's going on in the world today?

   c. If God is a God of love, why does he allow so many innocent people to suffer?

   d. Have you ever wondered about the future of our world?

   e. Do you have the personal assurance of eternal life? If you died tonight do you have the confidence you would live with Christ forever?

4. Suggest that the Bible provides answers to our deepest questions and to the deepest needs of the human heart.

5. Invite your new friend to begin a weekly series of Bible studies exploring the prophecies of the Bible for our time and answering the great questions of life.

Radio Church of God
(Herbert W. Armstrong group)

The name *Church of God* is used by more than 200 separate religious denominations in the United States. Fundamentally the names have been used to indicate that these churches have been gathered by the power of God and not retained the errors of the reform churches as they came out of Catholicism. They tend to emphasize the organizational practices of the New Testament church with particular emphasis on miracles, tongues, and the baptism of the Holy Spirit. The Church of God Seventh-day grew out of the Advent movement of the mid-1800's. It rejected the name Seventh-day Adventist when the Adventist Church was being organized from 1860-1863. A smaller group preferred the name Church of God. Herbert W. Armstrong left the Church of God Seventh-day in the 1930's to begin the Radio Church of God now known as the World-wide Church of God. Its *Plain Truth* magazine is circulated free to millions. The church also sponsors Ambassador College, and the Ambassador College Bible correspondence course.

Some doctrinal beliefs held in common with the Radio Church of God

1. Inspiration of the Bible.

2. The Second Coming of Christ.

3. The state of the dead and the annihilation of the wicked.

4. The acceptance of the Biblical health/dietary laws.

5. The keeping of the Seventh-day Sabbath.

6. The acceptance of the tithe principle.

Some major doctrinal misunderstandings of Radio Church of God and Bible texts to meet them

1. The belief that **Christ will reign on earth during the millennium** with the plagues poured out as punitive scourges to force the unsaved into submission.

   (See *Rev. 19:11-21; 20:1-10; Jn. 5:28,29; Jer. 4:23-26; 25:33.*) The word *Abussos* in *Rev. 20:1* is the same word as translated "Without form and void" in *Gen. 1:1,2* and *Jer. 4:23.* It means a place of desolation. For the precise time of the plagues see *Rev. 15:1,8; 16:12-21.*

2. The Radio Church of God **continues to observe the Jewish feasts** such as Passover, unleavened Bread, first fruits etc. On the 14th of *Nisan* in the Jewish calendar they observe Passover combined with a footwashing each year.

   (To show these feasts were fulfilled in Christ see *Col. 2:14-17; 1 Cor. 5:7,8; Gal. 4:1-11; 3:26-29.*)

3. The Radio Church of God believes that **Christ was crucified upon Wednesday,** due to the fact that Jesus said, "For as Jonas was three days and three nights in the of the whale's belly; so shall the Son of Man shall be in the heart of the earth for three days and nights" *(Jon. 1:17; Matt. 12:40.)*

   a. Jesus used a variety of expressions to describe His resurrection. He said *"in three days"* I will rise *(Matt. 26:61; 27:40; Mk. 14:58)*, and *"after three days"* *(Matt. 27:63; 12:40)*, and *the third day* *(Matt. 16:21; 17:23; 20:19; 27:64; Mk. 9:31; 10:34; Lk. 9:22; 18:33; 24:7,21,46).* The expressions "In three days" "after three days must be harmonized with the most common expression "the third day."

Jesus was resurrected not after three 24-hour periods but as He declared "the third day."

b. The common ancient method of counting was inclusive time reckoning. It included both the day upon which a particular period of time began and the day upon which it ended, no matter how small a fraction of the beginning or ending of the day was involved. The Bible lists several periods of three days which ended not after but during three days.

(See *Gen. 42:17-19; 1 Kings 12:5,12;* with *2 Chron. 10:5,12.)*

c. The clear Biblical evidence is that Jesus was crucified upon Friday and rose on Sunday.

(See *Mk. 16:9; Lk. 24:1,13,21,46; 23:54 to 24:1.)*

For extended coverage of this subject see the *Seventh-day Adventist Source Book,* vol. 9 of the *Commentary Series* pp. 248-251.

Possible approaches to Radio Church of God followers

1. Develop a close and strong friendship.

2. Share your testimony and personal relationship with Jesus. Many Armstrong followers have strong legalistic tendencies. Emphasize the "do's" of Christian experience. They need the assurance of salvation in Jesus.

   (1 Jn. 5:11,12; Jn. 1:12; Rom. 3:25-31; 6:14, 15; Eph. 2:8)

3. Study the significance of the three angels' messages. Most are fairly good Bible students and will respond well to a study on the deeper truths of *Revelation.*

4. When you approach topics like the millennium, keeping Jewish feasts, or the Wednes-

day crucifixion theory, do it with a tact borne of divine love.

5. The book, *What Adventists Believe,* our 27 fundamentals of faith is excellent for this group.

Secularists

Secularism is either the active pursuit of materialistic values in life or a philosophical view which dismisses God. To state it in negative terms: secularism is the lack of any apparent overt, visible interest in God, the Bible, religion, or spiritual values. Bible study, prayer, church attendance, and religious activities in general are unimportant. Money, fashion, material things, alcohol, drugs, sex, and sports have replaced God in the life of the secularist. The secularists motto is summed up in the words "Be Here Now!" translated, "enjoy life to the fullest." Secularists may be divided into at least four specific categories:

1. *The Secular Intellectual*—the scholarly type who has doubts about the inspiration of the Bible, the existence of God, and organized religion.

2. *The Secular Hard Hat*—the working class types or blue collar factory laborer who works hard all week and wants only to relax, drink beer, and watch the ball game on weekends.

3. *The Secular Religious Dropout*—the social activist type whose parents were members of organized churches, but who sees the church as irrelevant to contemporary needs. He is concerned with poverty, peace, racism, and social justice, but has little interest in God. Secularists are often interested in the moral ethic of Christianity but not the Christ of Christianity.

4. *The Secular Materialist*—the young urban professional type whose goals are a beautiful home, a high-paying job, a late model car, and exciting vacations. Material values are paramount in his life and possessions are his chief passion.

Possible approaches to the Secular Mind

Every human being responds to kindness. Genuine friendship breaks down prejudice. One thing is for certain, you will not win secularists to Christ by trying to out argue them. Every human being has felt needs in their life. These "felt needs" are areas where the individual senses a need for help. They might include the need for better health (quitting smoking, a low-fat diet, reduced stress, etc.), the need for a happier marriage, the need for a more satisfying job, the need for friendship, the need for understanding or even the need for forgiveness, freedom from guilt or inner peace. Look for areas in your secularist friend's life where he/she has these felt needs and attempt to meet them. Watch the walls of prejudice break down. Look for open doors of opportunity to share what Jesus personally means to you.

Three concrete approaches for secular people

1. Share the plan of salvation simply and lovingly:

   a. God created a perfect world *(Gen. 1:28)*.

   b. Adam and Eve lost the garden through sin *(Gen. 3:1-5)*.

   c. Sin separates us from God *(Isa. 59:1,2)*.

   d. The wages of sin is death *(Rom. 6:23)*.

   e. Since all have sinned all of us deserve to die eternally *(Rom. 3:23; 5:18)*.

   f. Through Jesus we can receive the gift of eternal life *(Jn. 3:16; Eph. 2:8; 2 Cor. 5:21)*.

2. Share some of the great Bible prophecies as evidence of the truthfulness of the Bible:

a. *Dan. 2*—Babylon, Medo-Persia, Greece, Rome, divisions of Rome, Jesus' coming.

b. Jesus birth place—Bethlehem *(Mic. 5:2).*

c. Cyrus named 150 years before his birth *(Isa. 44:28; 45:1,2).*

d. Prophecy of Tyre's destruction *(Ezek. 26:1-4, 19-21).*

e. Egypt desolate *(Ezek. 29:1-9).*

3. The third approach suggests that evolution is not a proven fact but a hypothesis. There are three scientific laws which evolution breaks:

a. Science declares life begets life. Evolution states given enough time, under the right conditions, non-living things will produce living things.

b. Science declares like produces like. Evolution says there are links in the gaps between kinds and species of animals. There is no concrete scientific evidence for such an assertion.

c. Science declares things left alone tend to break down (the second law of thermo dynamics). Evolution states things left alone tend to build up.

Only the Bible can present meaning to the great questions of life. Why am I here? Where did I come from? What is my future destiny? The Bible reveals a loving Christ made us. He will personally guide our lives. In Him we can be secure. Our eternal future is in His hands. Show your secular friend the hopelessness without God and the great joy in being secure in His hands.

Former Seventh-day Adventists

Research indicates that most former Adventists do not leave the church because of doctrinal reasons. Some do, but not the majority. Most leave because of one of the four following reasons:

1. A conflict with some other church member or their pastor.

2. A perception that the church is no longer relevant in their life and does not meet their needs.

3. Discouragement with themselves over a failure to live in harmony with church standards.

4. A growing disinterest in spiritual things in general due to a lack of adequate devotional and Bible study life.

When an individual misses church repeatedly for apparently no reason, there is an indication of spiritual trouble. If they are not immediately visited enabling them to discuss their spiritual problems, apostasy is likely to result. Warmth, friendliness and loving concern are often the agencies which God uses to stem the apostasy.

Signs that an individual may be growing discouraged and/or losing interest in the church.

1. Spasmodic church attendance/ lack of Prayer Meeting attendance.

2. A critical attitude, or general negative spirit.

3. A lack of spiritual fervor.

4. A return of old habit patterns (smoking, social drinking, worldly amusements).

5. A disregard for the Sabbath (T.V. watching Friday nights, shopping Sabbath afternoon, overtime work on Sabbath, etc.).

6. Estrangement from church members and/or failure to participate in the social life of the church.

Approaches to Former Adventists

1. Former Adventists usually do not need convincing regarding Adventist doctrines. They certainly do not need condemnation for their present life style. Don't be surprised or act shocked by their life style or habits. Most feel the pangs of a condemning conscience already. Further condemnation will only create hostility.

2. Demonstrate love, acceptance, and genuine concern.

3. Begin with topics of general interest by asking such questions as:

   a. Have you lived in this community for a number of years?

   b. Are you married or single? Do you have children?

   c. Do you work close to home? What is your occupation?

   These general questions provide a basis for getting acquainted in a non-threatening way. Ask them gently and lovingly with deep interest in the other person.

4. Proceed to topics of religious interest asking the following questions:

   a. I understand you used to attend the Seventh-day Adventist Church regularly, how long ago was that?

   b. Were you a member for a number of years?

   c. There are different reasons why people leave. Some experience disappointment in their own lives, others are hurt by church members or a pastor, still others feel the church doesn't meet their needs. Would you like to share with me why you no longer attend? I am really interested in knowing.

d. Listen carefully. Ask questions. Do not pass judgment on either the individual or the church. Make comments like, "I can understand why you might feel that way!"

e. After carefully listening, share what Jesus Christ means to you. Describe His incredible mercy, His marvelous forgiveness and His power to change lives. Use texts such as *Mic. 7:18,19; Heb. 8:12; 1 Jn. 1:9.* Emphasize the fact that, in the light of Jesus soon return, He is calling many of His former hurt children back to His church. Have prayer together and tell them you would like to see them again next week. Usually it is not wise to invite them back to church on the first visit. Each time an individual says no, it's easier to say no a second time.

f. Be sure to return after one week as you promised. Do not let your new friend down and squelch his/her new budding faith. On this second visit continue to listen. Share hopeful Bible promises such as *Ps. 32:8; 40:1,2;* and *Ps. 32:1,2.* Invite your new friend over for dinner. Share with them a copy of *Steps to Christ* particularly noting page 100 on God's wonderful love and desire to answer our prayers.

g. By your third visit plan to invite your new friend to some church program. I usually prefer inviting them to a social program or an evangelistic seminar or meeting before I invite them to the Sabbath morning church service. Offer to provide transportation. They will feel much more comfortable returning with you than alone.

5. On the fourth visit share positive comments from church members regarding their return. Let them know their former friends are really happy they are coming back. Personally encourage people who know them to call them by phone and express their joy at seeing them again. Invite them to church. Former S.D.A's are an extremely fruitful field for outstanding results. Generally they believe the Biblical message of Adventists. They have some friends already in the church. Disappointments, conflicts, or personal problems have led them away. They await a loving, caring, and genuine invitation to return.

Seventh-day Adventists have close historic ties with Seventh-day Baptists. A Seventh-day Baptist, Rachel Oaks Preston, shared the Sabbath truth with Joseph Bates who after careful Bible study accepted it. Early Millerite Adventists were Sunday-keepers until they re-studied the issue of the genuine Bible Sabbath after being introduced to it by Seventh-day Baptists. Bible-believing Baptist Christians kept the Sabbath truth alive in Europe throughout the reformation. They were first established in America in the late 17th century at Newport, Rhode Island. Their membership in the United States is approximately 5,000 today with a total world membership of close to 50,000. Administrative authority is centralized in a General Conference; however, each local congregation functions as an independent body having great freedom in both teachings and practice.

One of the major differences between Seventh-day Baptists and Seventh-day Adventists is prophetic urgency. Seventh-day Adventists see themselves as the prophetic remnant of *Rev. 12:17,* with a special commission from their Lord to herald the end-time message of *Rev. 14:6-12.* It is this last day message which has given evangelistic life to the advent movement enabling it to grow to a world-wide membership of seven million.

Some doctrinal beliefs held in common with Seventh-day Baptists

1. The Bible as the inspired Word of God.

2. The Trinity or Godhead.

3. The Virgin Birth.

4. Salvation through Christ alone.

5. The Seventh-day Sabbath.

6. Baptism by immersion.

7. The literal return of Christ (although some may accept the secret rapture).

8. A strong emphasis on religious liberty and freedom of conscience.

Some major doctrinal misunderstandings of Seventh-day Baptists and Bible texts to meet them

(Not all SDB's believe exactly as listed below, but most do.)

1. **Once saved always saved:** The belief that once an individual comes to Christ they can never lose their salvation.

   (See *1 Cor. 15:1,2; 2 Pet. 2:20-22; 1 Cor. 9:27* [The word castaway here is the same word used in *Jer. 6:30* for burned or rejected]; *Heb. 4:4-7; Rev. 3:5;* see also *Phil. 4:3*—When we accept Christ, our names are placed in the Book of Life. Since they can be removed, it is possible for those who once accepted to reject.)

2. **Immortality of the soul:** The belief that each individual has an immortal, indestructible soul distinct from the body but which leaves the body at death destined for heaven or hell.

   (See *1 Tim. 6:15,16; Gen. 2:7; Eccl. 12:7; Job 27:3; Ps. 146:4; 6:5; 115:17; Jn. 11:11-14.)* Remember the Bible uses the word "soul" 1,600 times and never *once* says "immortal soul." The Bible calls death a sleep 53 times.

3. **Eternal torment**: The belief that God punishes the lost in hell for eternity.

(See *Mal. 4:1-3; Ps. 37:10,11,20,38; Jude 7; 2 Pet. 2:6; Rev. 20:9; Heb. 12:29.*)

4. **The secret rapture:** The belief that Christ will return secretly prior to the tribulation (plagues) to snatch away or rapture His church leaving the unsaved on earth to suffer through the plagues.

(See *1 Thess. 4:16,17; 2 Thess. 1:7-9; 2:1-7; Matt. 13:30; 16:27; 24:27; Ps. 50:3; Rev. 1:7.*)

Possible approaches with Seventh-day Baptists

1. Establish agreement on the points we hold in common. Affirm your faith in and commitment to Jesus. Express your belief that salvation is by grace alone through faith.

2. Ask if they understand God's message for today as it is outlined in *Rev. 14:6-12.* Share your conviction that *Rev. 14* contains a message for our day as important as Noah's message was in his day. Suggest that you spend time together exploring the depths of the prophetic message.

3. Seventh-day Baptists do not accept the gift of prophecy as manifest in the writings of Ellen G. White. A Bible study on the role of the gift of prophecy in God's latter day movement utilizing such passages as *Eph. 4:8, and 11-15, 1 Cor. 1:6-8, Rev. 12:17, 19:10* and the tests of a true prophet found in *Deut. 13:1-4, Isa. 8:20, Dan. 10:17, Jer. 28:9,* and *Matt. 7:15* should eventually be given. I suggest avoiding the sensitive points with Seventh-day Baptists initially. Dwell on points we hold in common. Many Seventh-day Baptists will be fascinated with the prophecies of Daniel and *Revelation.* Something as straight forward as *Dan. 2* will excite your Seventh-day Baptist friends.

The Power of Intercessory Prayer

The principles in this volume are designed to enable you to become a more effective soul winner. People are won to Christ not merely by what we say but by the total impact of the Holy Spirit's working on their lives through us. Without the genuine infilling of the Holy Spirit, our words will be ineffective.

Mark's Gospel describes Jesus' incredible power as a soulwinner. The masses were amazed declaring, "He teaches as one having authority and not as the scribes" *(Mk. 1:22)*. The secret of Jesus soulwinning power is found in *verse 35*, "And in the morning rising up a great while before day, he went out and departed into a solitary place and there prayed."

The secret of Jesus' power was the secret of intercessory prayer. If you want to be a soul winner, heaven's power will come as on your knees you pray for individual people. As we pray for others, God grants us wisdom to reach them (Jas. 1:5). He gives us the keys to their hearts. As we pray, through the influence of the Holy Spirit, God works upon their hearts in ways He could not if we did not pray.

In the great controversy between good and evil in the universe, God respects human freedom. He gives each of His children the opportunity to choose. Through angels, the influence of the Holy Spirit and the providential circumstances of life, God is doing everything He can without violating human freedom to win individuals to Himself.

When we hold up specific individuals before God in intercessory prayer, respecting our freedom, He pours out His Holy Spirit through us to reach them. We become channels of His influence—we become conduits of

His power. The water of life flows from the throne of God to thirsty souls through us. In the conflict between good and evil, "God will do in answer to the prayer of faith that which He would not do, did we not thus ask" (*Great Controversy*, p. 525).

The section below provides an opportunity for you to become an intercessor. In the left column write the name of the person you are praying for, or the special request you have before God. In the right column record God's answer. Read these promises regularly to strengthen your faith: *Matt. 7:7; Mk. 11:24; 1 Jn. 5:16.*

Prayer Diary

Prayer Request	**God's Answer**